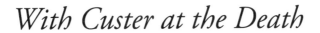

With Custer at the Death

Lieutenant-Colonel George Armstrong Custer
Commanding 7TH CAVALRY

With Custer at the Death
A Tactical Analysis of the
Battle of the Little Bighorn

Robert F. Burke

Strategy & Tactics Press
Bakersfield, California

To the memory of Robert F. Burke
from his loving family.
He was dedicated to Truth.

————————————————✕————————————————

Published by
Strategy & Tactics Press
PO Box 21598
Bakersfield CA 93390
661/587-9633 • fax: 661/587-5031
www.strategyandtacticspress.com

Printed in the United States of America

ISBN: 978-0-9823343-2-4
Library of Congress Control Number: 2010928419
p. 112, cm. 30

Contents

Map Notes

Terrain features generally are presented with standard symbols. The elevations give only an indication of relative altitude and should not be viewed as steep slopes; for the most part, the battlefield consisted of gently rolling hills. The valley floor sits at approximately 3000 feet above sea level, with contours presented at 100 foot increments. The notation has been omitted from the maps for the sake of clarity. See *Appendix II* for a description of place names on the maps.

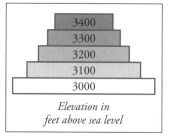

3400
3300
3200
3100
3000

Elevation in feet above sea level

 Wolf Tooth   Indian War Party

 Cavalry Troop
(mounted & general display)

 Cavalry Troop
(dismounted in firing line)

 Cavalry Battalion

 Cavalry Regiment

Cavalry units are presented in dark gray boxes using traditional military symbology. The trace lines are used when the units formed dismounted firing lines for long periods. Troops are identified by letter; when known, platoons are identified by number (using the assumption that the senior officer in each troop would command the *1st Platoon*).

Indian war parties are displayed in white as a general shape, as they did not form tight formations like the cavalry but fought in a loose mass of individuals. Where known, each party is identified by the name of the primary chief.

All maps and diagrams by Christopher Perello after originals by the author. Minor changes have been made to the originals, particularly regarding time notations, to conform the maps to the text.

List of Maps

Foreword

For decades, surveys have shown the Battle of the Little Bighorn is one of the most well known events in American history. There's a disturbing characteristic, though, to that high level of recognition. That is, the battle's place in the popular imagination seems to be based largely on the repeated tellings offered in numerous Hollywood and made-for-TV movies, as well as shorter presentations given the fight in various western-based television series of the late 1950s and early 1960s. From those sources, the impression's been created George Armstrong Custer was no more than a blundering, blustering oaf, who vaingloriously ordered his men to certain doom, against all military logic, all in the hope of his eventually being elected president or some such.

The course of the battle, as shown in those sources, general goes no further than to show Custer stupidly charging into the huge Indian village, and then registering his shock and surprise in close-up. That's quickly followed by a single and immediately overwhelming Indian counterattack, which succeeds in overrunning all of the Custer Battalion in one swift and seamless effort, all usually before the end of the reel or the next commercial break.

The scholarly reinterpretations of the battle, many of which are based on archaeological findings at the battle site, and which began appearing in the 1970s, have also largely failed on two counts. First, some of them seem to have as their primary purpose little more than putting forward a politically correct view of the of the battle: what might be termed the 'poor Native-American freedom-fighters vs. the Nazi-analog-cavalry' school of interpretation. Second, being intellec-

tual endeavors offered in a society that's often broadly described as being anti-intellectual, the reach of those new efforts hasn't been nearly as broad as those of of the movie and television industry (the occasional special on such under-viewed TV "networks" as the "History Channel" aside).

This book is meant as a corrective to all that. It's presented for those who'd like to study and understand the Battle of the Little Bighorn as just what it was: a significant cavalry engagement that was fought over the course of seven hours across an area of more than 23 square miles.

In author Burke's smooth account – one that's supported by what I believe to be easily the best collection of maps available anywhere on this topic – the reader will learn Custer tried no fewer than four major offensive efforts to win the battle, at one point came close to escaping with most of his command still intact and, even when forced permanently onto the defensive, still kept determinedly maneuvering until near the very end. Likewise, the Indians are shown to have done much more than simply charge in 'a hootin' and a hollerin.' They had a command structure, used diverse tactics at different times during the battle, and several times had to pause to regroup and reassess the evolving situation before finally being able to close in and finish off the bluecoats.

The *Prologue* and *Epilogue*, drawn from a magazine article Joseph Miranda, longtime editor of *Strategy & Tactics,* explain the larger context in which the battle took place.

Those interested in the actual study and discussion of military history, then, are in for a treat – enjoy.

Ty Bomba
Senior Editor
Strategy & Tactics Press

Prologue
Through Noon on 25 June 1876

This chapter is an excerpt from
The Little Bighorn-Yellowstone Campaign of 1876
by Joseph Miranda
first published in Strategy & Tactics #236

our centuries passed between the landing of Christopher Columbus in the New World and the United States Census Bureau's official announcement of the closing of the frontier in 1890. That period saw a dramatic struggle in which European peoples colonized North America and created new nations from the Atlantic to the Pacific. The most dramatic change occurred in the last of the four centuries.

At the time of the establishment of the United States of America in 1787, the country consisted mainly of settled territories along the Atlantic seaboard with claimed territory staked out to the west. Powerful Indian nations held sway west of the Appalachians and could even threaten the "civilized" regions to the east with frequent raids. Indian fighting prowess had been legendary since British colonists had first landed in the New World. These were warrior cultures, fully adapted to the conditions of fighting in the terrain in which they operated. In fact, European armies learned much from the Indians about irregular warfare and light infantry tactics. The reverse also was true: unlike many other "native" peoples encountered by the Europeans

in the age of imperialism, the Indians were quick to adapt to the use of firearms. Yet within a century, the United States would defeat all the Indian peoples and consolidate control of the continent. The question, then, is why, given the advantages the Indians held, did the white man win at all?

The essential problem with the Indians was their lack of unity, which had been endemic since before Europeans first landed in the Americas. In the sixteenth century, Hernan Cortez exploited the division among the Mexican Indians by supporting rebellious tribes fighting to overthrow the Aztec Empire. Similarly, as Britain and then the United States expanded from the Atlantic coast westward, the Europeans faced numerous Indian nations, who generally were unable to act collectively.

On those rare occasions when the Indians did unite, they often proved more than a match for "modern" armies. In 1790-91, the Indians of the Ohio Valley defeated two small U.S. armies in the old Northwest, though the final victory went to Gen. "Mad" Anthony

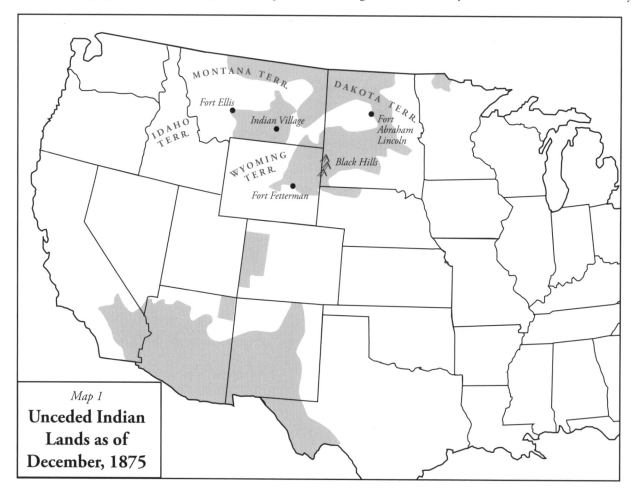

Map 1
Unceded Indian Lands as of December, 1875

Wayne in 1794 at Fallen Timbers. In 1811 Tecumseh's confederation of northwest Indians gave the U.S. serious concern until William Harrison defeated him at Tippecanoe. The Seminoles carried out decades of guerrilla warfare in Florida. As late as the War of 1812, there was also the possibility of gaining support from colonial powers (such as Britain), who saw the Indians as a force balancing the expanding United States.

The Indians, though, proved capable of uniting only under a unique set of circumstances. One was when great leaders, such as Tecumseh, came to the fore. Another was when the westward movement of whites was simply too great to ignore.

By the time of the American Civil War, the continent east of the Mississippi had been largely settled and tied into the growing industrial revolution with factories and railroads. The U.S. was poised to move into the Great Plains. Many of the Plains Indians, such as the Sioux, were themselves newcomers west of the Mississippi, having been pushed westward in previous centuries by other Indian peoples. They adapted well to a nomadic existence, however, using the horse for mobility and basing their economy on hunting buffalo.

By the 1870s, the U.S. migration into the plains was overwhelming, spurred by a combination of gold rush, railroad building and buffalo hunting. In the wake of these rushes came settlers, who built farms and towns. These land grabs pushed the Indians into ever smaller tracts, limiting their mobility and destroying the buffalo herds.

Events in the Dakota Territory came to a head in 1875. The discovery of gold a year earlier in the Black Hills had ignited a frenzied rush of whites into the area. The army tried, but could not stop the invasion. At the same time, the Grant administration came under intense pressure to find a way to open the area to settlement.

The solution was found in the fact that portions of several tribes refused to relocate to specified agencies (reservations). An ultimatum was issued requiring all Indians to report to the agencies by the end of 1875.

Lakota (Sioux) and Cheyenne war chiefs such as Crazy Horse and Gall, seeing the crisis, mobilized large numbers of warriors for the confrontation. Spiritual leaders such as Sitting Bull provided additional cement to a growing confederation of tribes. By the end of the year, an unprecedented number of Indians had collected along the Little Bighorn River in what is now southeastern Montana. It was against this concentration the army would move.

Militarily, the Army had several advantages on what today would be termed the strategic and operational levels of war. The most obvious one was political. The United States was a single unified state. Even the Civil War did not impede western expansion. If anything, it provided an impetus for the Union to build a transcontinental railroad. More than any other factor, it was the railroad that opened the west to a burgeoning eastern population, equipped with all the tools and trappings of the industrial revolution, including a well-equipped army.

In addition to the rapid movement of men, railroads gave the Army one of its chief advantages: its logistical tail. Units took the field accompanied by supply wagons, pack mule trains, and herds of cattle for meat on the hoof. They were guaranteed a consistent supply of ammunition and food (despite the usual losses due to corruption) kept in depots and forts. These posts also provided safe havens to regroup and refit tired forces. The Army thus could campaign year round. Indians generally became inactive during winter as the lack of grazing grasses hobbled their horses.

Other technological advances included ever-more powerful weapons and modern communications. The telegraph allowed almost instantaneous transmission of information and plans. Significantly, the 1876 campaign was fought largely beyond the reach of the railroad and telegraph, and much of the American difficulties came from the inability to coordinate widely separated columns.

The Indians had no equivalent to a regular "army." Warbands were formed around prominent leaders, and those chiefs had no means with which to maintain the individual warrior's participation in a campaign other than through strength of personality. Tribal decisions were made by consensus and a rough kind of democracy.

The closest the Indians came to a standing military were warrior societies, or *akicitas*, which selected proven individuals and took the lead in combat. One of the more famous of those societies originated with the Cheyenne as the Hotamintanto, usually translated as "dog soldiers." Strengths were in stealth, tracking, and fighting as an individual with a variety of weapons. These often included modern rifles, even repeaters, though they lacked sufficient ammunition to make sustained campaigning practical.

On occasion, Indians could cooperate effectively in battle. However, the warrior tradition stressed indi-

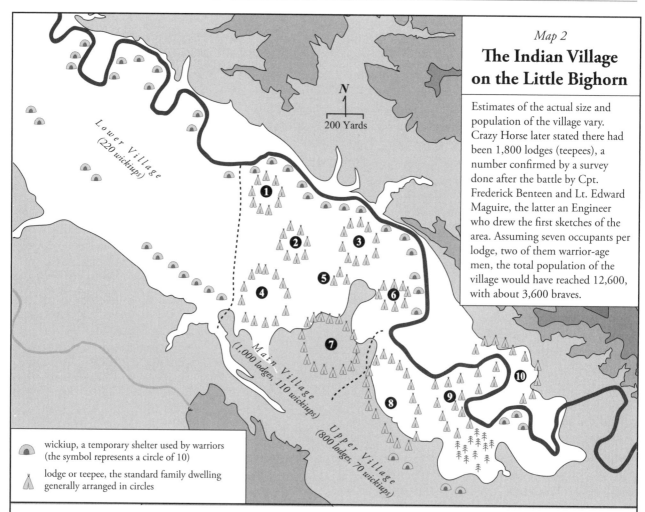

Map 2
The Indian Village on the Little Bighorn

Estimates of the actual size and population of the village vary. Crazy Horse later stated there had been 1,800 lodges (teepees), a number confirmed by a survey done after the battle by Cpt. Frederick Benteen and Lt. Edward Maguire, the latter an Engineer who drew the first sketches of the area. Assuming seven occupants per lodge, two of them warrior-age men, the total population of the village would have reached 12,600, with about 3,600 braves.

wickiup, a temporary shelter used by warriors (the symbol represents a circle of 10)

lodge or teepee, the standard family dwelling generally arranged in circles

	Tribal Affiliation	Lodges	Estimated Warriors	Head Chief	War Chief (Sub-Chiefs)
❶	Non-Agency Cheyenne Circle	122	240	Ice Bear	Two Moon (Wooden Leg, Yellow Nose, Comes in Sight)
❷	Brule Circle	69	136	Crow Dog	Little Hawk (Iron Star)
❸	Sans Arc Circle	110	220	Spotted Eagle	Black Eagle (White Bull, Circling Bear)
❹	Non-Agency Oglala Circle	240	480	Old Man Afraid	Crazy Horse (He Dog, Foolish Elk, No Water)
❺	Lodges of the Great Council & the Warrior Societies				
❻	Minniconju Circle	168			
	Minniconju		300	Lame Deer	Fast Bull (Hump, American Horse, Red Horse)
	Two Kettle		36	Runs the Enemy	Runs the Enemy
❼	Blackfoot Circle	291	582	Scabby Head	Kill Eagle (Jumping Bear)
❽	Hunkpapa Circle	395			
	Hunkpapa		720	Sitting Bull	Gall (Crow King, Rain in the Face, One Bull)
	Santee		40	Inapaduta	
	Yankton		30	-	
❾	Agency Cheyenne Circle	180	360	Dirty Moccasin	Lame White Man (Little Horse, Old Man Coyote)
❿	Agency Oglala Circle	225	450	Big Head	Low Dog (Big Road)

Also present were hunting parties of Arapahoe (5 men) and Gros Ventres (2 men), who lodged with the Non-Agency Cheyenne, and , Assiniboins (2 men), who lodged with the Brule. Approximately one-quarter of the total estimated warriors were elders, capable only of defending the village proper. Of the active braves, nearly 300 were not in the village when Custer arrived in the afternoon of 25 June, leaving an estimated 2,300 men available to meet the cavalry attack.

vidual fighting prowess. Often, symbolic acts of bravery, such as counting coup (striking an opponent with a ceremonial staff) were considered more important than winning a battle.

Actions were fought largely as raids and skirmishes to seize horses and captives, to settle scores, and to establish the reputation of individuals and tribes. That philosophy carried through to the Indians' confrontations with the white intruders. Most of the actions fought by hostile Indians or Army forces amounted to raids on small outposts or isolated settlements. The Hollywood image of Indians attacking wagon trains is largely a myth; the usual Indian "policy" was to allow the settlers to move through their territory and let the next tribe worry about them.

"Indian fighting" encompassed violations of contemporary standards of civilized warfare. During the Lakota uprising of 1862 in Minnesota, the Sioux killed several hundred civilians. U.S. reprisals could be equally savage (though often giving rise to public outrage): at Sand Creek (29 November 1864), Colonel John Chivington and three regiments of volunteers massacred a village of peaceful Indians. At the Washita (27 November 1868), George Armstrong Custer and the *7TH CAVALRY* attacked a Cheyenne village (which this time around was not quite as peaceful).

Such large actions were the exception. The Indians were possessed of superb mobility, making it difficult to bring them to battle unless they chose. Tied to no permanent structures, entire villages could be dismantled and stowed on *travois* towed by horses. Even with accompanying "civilians," a tribe could move up to 50 miles a day, more than double the Army's speed.

The Indians did have a number of vulnerabilities. The generally disjointed nature of Indian warfare precluded long-range strategic planning. The lack of any command hierarchy meant onerous duties like posting pickets and sentries could not be enforced.

Probably the greatest weakness was the complete lack of a logistical base. The Indians simply could not operate in winter owing to lack of forage and the attrition engendered by snow and freezing temperatures – the negative side of their high mobility.

Army leaders with experience on the plains understood those vulnerabilities and realized that to win they would have to attack the Indians where they were weakest. Consequently, sneak attacks on Indian encampments, and sustained winter campaigns, became viable and necessary alternatives. Also useful were raids to seize Indian horse herds, since without their mounts,

the warriors could not fight effectively and the villages could not move. Gen. Crook, a veteran Indian fighter, launched his part of the 1876 campaign in February to exploit the winter conditions, though he still ended up repulsed at the Powder River (17 March). Custer's primary objective at the Washita was to destroy Indian supplies and horses, thereby forcing the Indians to move back to the reservation.

The Army was heading toward total war, while the Indians were desperately trying to make the old ways work. Essentially, the Indians avoided anything approaching what might be otherwise defined as a "battle." Even if their tribal and military organization had made such fights possible, they could not afford

---

Battles of the Indian Wars

Until the 1876 campaign there were perhaps a half-dozen actions on the Plains that remotely could be considered "battles" in the "civilized" understanding of the word.

The Beecher Island Fight (Colorado, 17 September 1866): Fifty Army scouts were attacked by about 1,000 Indians. The scouts, armed with repeaters, held out until relieved.

The Fetterman Fight (Wyoming, 21 December 1866): Chiefs Red Cloud and Crazy Horse, with 1,500 Sioux and Cheyenne, wiped out Capt. William Fetterman and his command of 80 men. As a result, government forces temporarily withdrew from Wyoming and promised the Black Hills to the Sioux in perpetuity. It was a war the Indians effectively, won.

The Wagon Box Fight (Wyoming, 2 August 1867): A 1,000-man band of Sioux was thrown back by a 32-man Army woodcutting detail armed with repeating rifles. This action inspired a painting of the event that has since decorated orderly rooms throughout the US Army.

The Washita River (Oklahoma, 27 November 1868): Custer led the *7TH CAVALRY* in an attack against an Indian village. Resistance was strong, with about 150 warriors and some women returning fire.

Summit Springs (Colorado, 11 July 1869): Col. Eugene Carr, with eight companies of the *5TH CAVALRY* and some Pawnee scouts, scattered a contingent of Cheyenne dog soldiers.

Palo Duro (Texas, 28 September 1874): Col. R.S. Mackenzie and the *4TH CAVALRY* charged a band of Comanches, Kiowa, and Cheyenne who were holed up in a canyon. Mackenzie's troopers succeeded in destroying the Indians' supplies, which made it impossible for them to continue fighting in the coming winter.

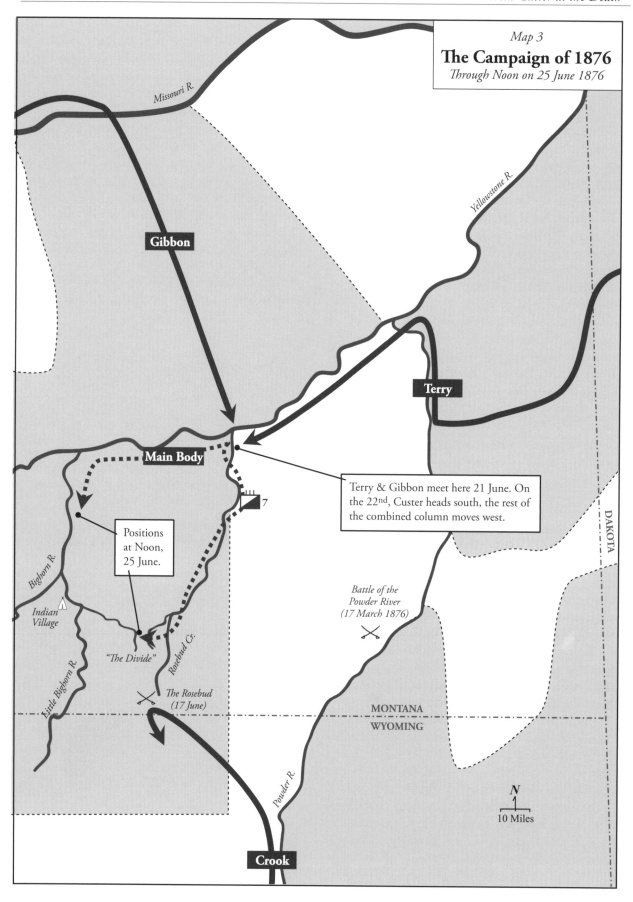

Map 3
The Campaign of 1876
Through Noon on 25 June 1876

Gibbon

Yellowstone R.

Missouri R.

Terry

Main Body

7

Terry & Gibbon meet here 21 June. On the 22nd, Custer heads south, the rest of the combined column moves west.

Positions at Noon, 25 June.

DAKOTA

Bighorn R.

Battle of the Powder River (17 March 1876)

Indian Village

"The Divide"

Rosebud Cr.

Little Bighorn R.

The Rosebud (17 June)

MONTANA
WYOMING

Powder R.

N
10 Miles

Crook

the losses that even a victory would entail. The mass casualties sustained by European and U.S. armies in the French and Indian War, the American Revolution, the War of 1812, and especially the Civil War, would have been incomprehensible (not to mention suicidal) to the Plains Indians. That would change in 1876, but the change came as a surprise to the army, and more pointedly to Custer and the men of the *7TH CAVALRY*.

The campaign got underway before the winter snows had melted. Three small forces were to converge on the various Indian bands roaming eastern Montana. Brig. Gen. Alfred H. Terry, commander of the Army's *Department of Dakota*, had overall command of the campaign. One, including the *7TH CAVALRY*, was under his immediate command and would operate from Fort Abraham Lincoln in the Dakota Territory. The second, under Col. John Gibbon, would start at Fort Ellis, near present-day Bozeman, Montana. The third column, commanded by Brig. Gen. George Crook, was to march up from Fort Fetterman in the Wyoming Territory. The idea was to trap the Indians between the three columns so they could not move farther onto the Plains. The Army could then defeat the "hostiles" or force them back to the reservations.

Seen from a conventional military standpoint, Terry forces were badly divided. The Dakota and Montana Columns had about 1,000 and 500 men, respectively, and Crook's force was not much larger. Between all three there were but five Gatling guns and two cannon. Effectively, the strength of a single Civil War brigade was about to take on nearly 6,000 warriors; the Army had estimated considerably fewer. Even so, a practiced military eye could see the Indians had the advantage of central position. Conceivably, the Indians could concentrate against each of the three columns to defeat them in detail.

The Army did not think the Indians capable of such coordinated maneuvers. Given past experience, Terry had every reason to expect the Indians would break off and withdraw farther into the plains. The problem as he saw it was not in fighting the Indians — the belief was that disciplined soldiers with breechloading weapons could hold off any number of warriors — but in finding and fixing the hostiles.

Things did not go according to plan. An early foray by Crook was repulsed at the Powder River in March. The main campaign got underway in June, with all three columns on the move simultaneously.

Once again, the Indians upset the Army's calculations. They were fighting as they had never fought before and would never fight again: as a cohesive force. Why they chose to fight that way is a matter for conjecture. No doubt it was in part owing to the rise of great chiefs such as Crazy Horse and Gall, who appear to have had a conception of how their Army opponents operated. The Sand Creek Massacre had convinced many Indians peaceful accommodation would not work. There was also the desperation factor, with the Indians not only losing the last of their great hunting ranges but also being hemmed in from all sides by the Army.

In a maneuver that would have made Napoleon proud, Crazy Horse invoked his interior lines. He first led his warriors against Crook along the Rosebud Creek. As had happened at the Powder River, Crook's command was fought to a standstill (17 June). U.S. casualties were light, but Crook's position was untenable. Facing strong enemy forces and reliant on a long and vulnerable supply line, he had to withdraw.

Just four days later and 100 miles to the north, the columns under Terry and Gibbon united on the Yellowstone River. Able to move only at the pace of a marching man, Terry feared the Indians would slip away. The next day, he ordered Custer to take his *7TH CAVALRY* and ride ahead in what would today be called a reconnaissance in force.

Custer was to move south (toward the presumed location of Crook's column), then turn back north, driving the Indians in front of him and into the combined Terry-Gibbon column. So trapped, the Indians could be finally brought to battle and, presumably, defeated. Terry, no doubt, envisioned he would win the decisive victory on the plains that had so long evaded other Army commanders.

Custer drove forward for two days, reaching the confluence of the Davis and Rosebud Creeks. His plan had been to rest his men on 25 June, while scouts ascertained the exact location of the Indian encampment. The following day, Custer would launch a surprise attack on the Indians in conjunction with Terry, who had taken a more direct route.

However, there were signs that the *7TH CAVALRY* had been spotted by Indian scouts. If he had, the Indian encampment surely would be warned. Resting would give the Indians a full day to get on the move, and the Army columns would converge on empty space. Though his men and horses were tired, Custer felt he had no choice but to push on.

Chapter One
Movement to Contact
Noon - 2:56 p.m.

It was nearly mid-afternoon on a hot Sabbath day, 25 June 1876, when troopers of the U.S. *7TH CAV-ALRY REGIMENT,* led by George Armstrong Custer, reached the south bank of North Fork Creek. There, at a minor tributary of the Little Bighorn River, which ran about a mile to the west, Custer dismounted his command to allow the men to water their horses and fill their canteens.

The general (Custer's real rank was Lieutenant Colonel, but he had received a temporary rank of Major General during the Civil War and was called "general" as a matter of courtesy) was about to embark on the greatest gamble of his tempestuous 15-year military career. His brazen Civil War exploits and repeated successes against the Indians of the west had made his a household name. Now, in the wilds of south-central Montana, the one-time "Boy General" sensed this was to be another history making campaign.

Mark Kellogg, a journalist, was along to record it for posterity, despite the fact Custer had been specifically ordered not to take anyone from that profession. Assigned by the *Bismarck Tribune* as a "special correspondent," Kellogg was also anticipating events that would give him a spectacular scoop, perhaps a great clash with the largest concentration of Indian hostiles ever seen. He had written what would turn out to be his final dispatch just a few days earlier: *"We leave for the Rosebud tomorrow, and by the time this reaches you we will have met and fought the Red Devils; with what result remains to be seen. I go with Custer and will be at the death."*

Custer retained command of only a portion of his 650-man regiment. Once the decision to move forward had been made that morning, the entire regiment had pressed forward quickly. Shortly after noon, the column reached the summit (or "divide") of a low mountain range 11 miles from the Little Bighorn.

There, Custer divided the regiment, Capt. Thomas M. McDougall's *B TROOP* was assigned to protect the 160 supply- and ammunition-laden mules of the pack train, The remaining 11 troops were formed into three battalions, temporary formations used to simplify command and control in the field. Three troops each went to Custer's second-in-command, Maj. Marcus A. Reno and to Capt. Frederick W. Benteen. The remaining five, with the regimental headquarters detachment, formed Custer's battalion of 227 men: 217 soldiers, seven scouts and three civilians.

Having been compelled by circumstance into starting a premature action in unfamiliar territory, and certain only that the hostiles were somewhere nearby, Custer now began to improvise. He ordered Benteen to circle to the southwest to prevent the Indians using the area, either for escape or attack. He and Reno — preceded by scouting parties and trailed by McDougall's slow moving pack train — were to advance west along Upper Ash Creek. That was a relatively level stretch of ground flanked on both sides by vast expanses of rugged terrain (which Benteen's men would have to traverse).

By 2:43 p.m. Custer had reached the vicinity of what has since been called the "Flat," a tongue of bottom-land terminating at its western end in a low knoll that was quickly occupied by the scouts. Though he did not yet know its precise location, the center of the encampment he long had been seeking lay just four miles to the northwest. As he arrived at the knoll, Custer was informed a large formation of hostiles had been seen riding away, in apparent flight, toward the Little Bighorn valley. Fearing a mass exodus was already underway, Custer told Reno to take his battalion and most of the scouts to attack from the south, via the Upper Valley Ford. Custer himself would advance some distance behind Reno.

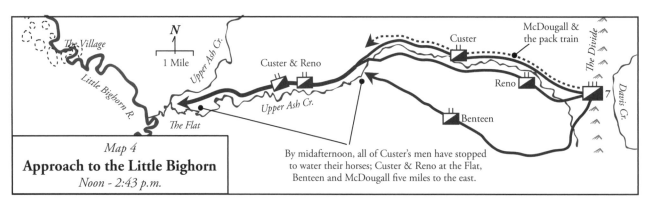

Map 4
Approach to the Little Bighorn
Noon - 2:43 p.m.

By midafternoon, all of Custer's men have stopped to water their horses; Custer & Reno at the Flat, Benteen and McDougall five miles to the east.

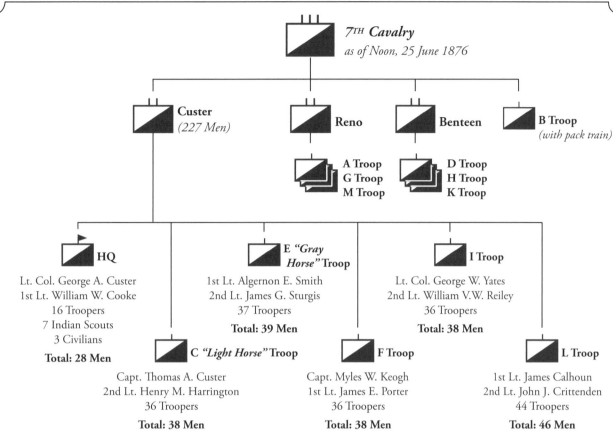

7TH Cavalry
as of Noon, 25 June 1876

Custer
(227 Men)

Reno

Benteen

B Troop
(with pack train)

A Troop
G Troop
M Troop

D Troop
H Troop
K Troop

HQ
Lt. Col. George A. Custer
1st Lt. William W. Cooke
16 Troopers
7 Indian Scouts
3 Civilians
Total: 28 Men

E "Gray Horse" Troop
1st Lt. Algernon E. Smith
2nd Lt. James G. Sturgis
37 Troopers
Total: 39 Men

I Troop
Lt. Col. George W. Yates
2nd Lt. William V.W. Reiley
36 Troopers
Total: 38 Men

C "Light Horse" Troop
Capt. Thomas A. Custer
2nd Lt. Henry M. Harrington
36 Troopers
Total: 38 Men

F Troop
Capt. Myles W. Keogh
1st Lt. James E. Porter
36 Troopers
Total: 38 Men

L Troop
1st Lt. James Calhoun
2nd Lt. John J. Crittenden
44 Troopers
Total: 46 Men

• As far as can be known, this chart depicts the *7TH Cavalry* at the time it reached "The Flat."

• The *7TH CAVALRY* was present in its entirety, a rarity for units on the Plains. There was no *"J TROOP"* to avoid typographic confusion with *I*.

• The nicknames of *C* and *E TROOPS* derived from the uniform color of their horses; the mounts of the other troops were Colorado Bay ("Blood Brown").

• In the field, troops (also called companies, though the latter term applied to all branches of the army, while "troop" was exclusive to the cavalry) were divided into two platoons, either of which could be commanded by either company officer. For this narrative, absent specific information, the assumption is that the senior officer always commanded the *1ST PLATOON*.

• The relatively uniform strength of the troops suggests that cross-leveling – moving men from larger troops to smaller ones – had been done, either before the campaign or while in the field.

The cavalry's primary weapon was the single shot breechloading Springfield Model 1873 carbine. It had a much faster rate of fire than pre-war muzzle loaders, twice the range of most repeating rifles (including those carried by many of the Indians at the Little Bighorn) and an even gerater range advantage over bows. Officers had some latitude in choosing their own weapons, and Custer brought along a Remington hunting rifle in 1876.

It had been chosen as much for ease of amintenance as for performance. After-battle reports that it jammed easily do not stand up to investigation; likely the story -was circulated as an explanation for the cavalry defeat.

In addition to the carbine, troopers carried a Model 1873 Colt revolver. This was a heavy, powerful handgun, easy to use on horseback and highly effective at close range and in swirling mounted melees.

A saber also was issued to cavalrymen. Oddly enough, cavalry charges with saber and pistol often proved effective in surprise attacks on Indian villages. This likely was due more to the surprise and to the physical weight of well-fed cavalry mounts in tight formation than to the weapon itself. Certainly the saber faired poorly against Indian bows in a mounted fight. In any case, the blades were left behind for the 1876 campaign.

The regimental adjutant, Lieutenant William W. Cooke, was assigned the task of keeping Custer apprised of Reno's progress. The commander of *I Troop*, Captain Myles W. Keogh, and two of his men, Privates John Mitchell and Archibald McIllhargey, briefly accompanied Cooke.

Though Custer specifically promised to support the major, Reno soon found himself on his own. The general saw a group of about 100 mounted warriors on some high ground to the right, and Custer instantly decided to shift his force in that direction, which took him to the edge of North Fork Creek, behind the knoll. There dense thickets of cottonwood trees and brush concealed his presence from anyone in the valley, though not from two tribesmen who happened to be on the bluffs before him. One of those had journeyed down to the creek a few minutes earlier, and on seeing Custer approach had quickly turned around.

Custer dispatched a five-man detail from *F Troop*, on the right, to probe the high ground ahead. He also sent a party of Crow scouts, on the left, toward a barrier of sheer cliffs overlooking the river. On their return, the Crows' half-breed interpreter, Mitch Boyer,

told Custer there was no evidence of any large bands of Indians in the valley; nor for that matter was there any sign of Sitting Bull's encampment. To Custer that meant only one thing: having been forewarned of his presence, the renegades were in full flight, and he must act quickly to prevent their escape.

Scanning the unknown upland ahead of him, it seemed logical there had to be an alternative route by which to enter the broad flood plain of the Little Bighorn and there come to grips with the enemy. Thus it happened that, with Reno about to engage and neither Benteen nor McDougall anywhere in sight, Custer decided the moment had come to strike. He gave the order and his men scrambled to reform their units; the column order of each being determined entirely by the time it took them to saddle-up.

As they did so, Custer bent down on one knee, hat in hand, head bowed in a moment of silent prayer, while Boyer and the scouts stood nearby in silence. Then he stood up, walked over to them and solemnly shook hands with each, thanking them individually for having safely led him to that place. It was just as the impromptu ceremony was finishing that Capt. Ke-

Major Marcus J. Reno
Regimental Major, 7th Cavalry

Captain Frederick W. Benteen
Commanding H Troop, 7th Cavalry
(detached as battalion commander)

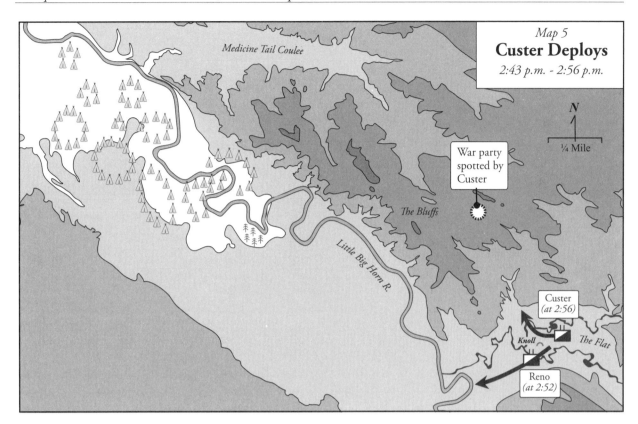

ogh rode in with news Reno's men were crossing the Little Bighorn without meeting resistance. The general seemed pleased and, pointing to a large cloud of billowing dust some distance off, remarked: *"Keogh, those Indians are running. If we can keep them at it, we can afford to sacrifice half the horses in the command."*

The ever-observant Custer knew some of his men and animals were tired to the point of exhaustion. He had led them more than 22 miles during the previous 15 hours and, despite two halts, the harsh climate and high temperatures made it difficult to get proper rest. That, plus the cumulative effects of nearly six weeks of campaigning, had taken a toll. Though Custer himself — a man of extraordinary endurance and athletic ability — seemed impervious to all of it, he appreciated

his men's situation. Still, he was not worried. In spite of everything, morale remained high; the troops were ready and eager to get on with the job at hand.

The regiment was thus committed and, as Keogh returned to his own troop, Custer and the Crow scouts mounted and took their places with the headquarters personnel at the front of the column. After looking behind him and seeing all was ready, Custer said to Boyer: *"Now take a look-see from that near ridge and find out how things stand from there."*

Boyer relayed the order to Half Yellow Face, the real leader of the Crow, who obediently moved out accompanied by White Swan. As the two scouts spurred their ponies, the battalion began to move forward. It was 2:56 p.m.

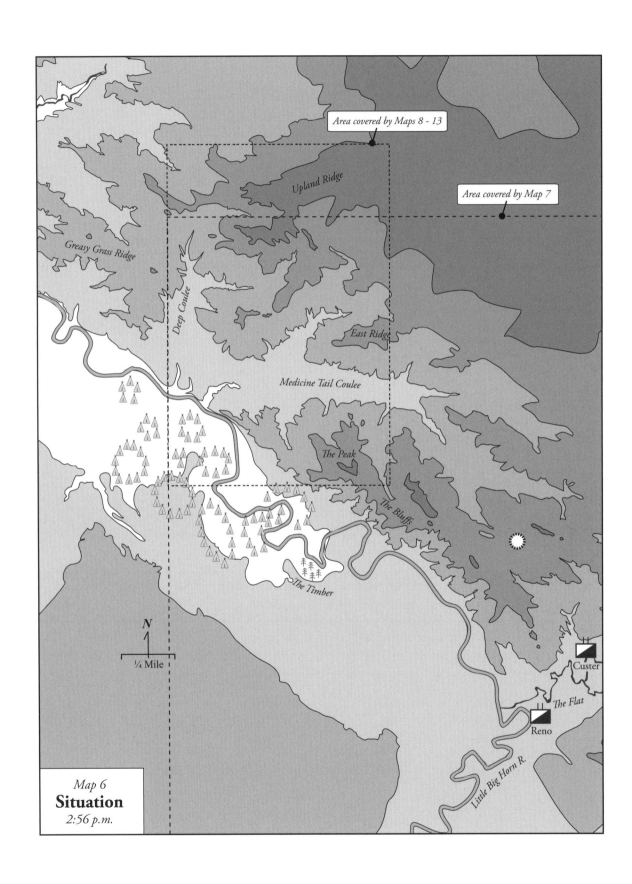

Area covered by Maps 8 - 13

Area covered by Map 7

Upland Ridge

Greasy Grass Ridge

Deep Coulee

East Ridge

Medicine Tail Coulee

The Peak

The Bluffs

The Timber

Custer

The Flat

Reno

Little Big Horn R.

N

¼ Mile

Map 6
Situation
2:56 p.m.

Chapter Two
Medicine Tail Ford
2:56 p.m. - 4:13 p.m.

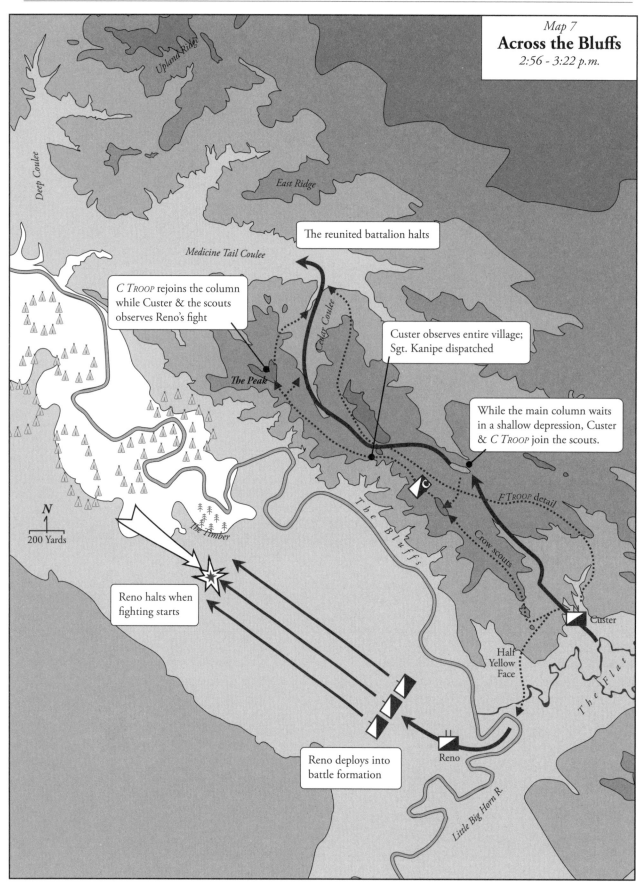

Map 7
Across the Bluffs
2:56 - 3:22 p.m.

The reunited battalion halts

C Troop rejoins the column while Custer & the scouts observes Reno's fight

Custer observes entire village; Sgt. Kanipe dispatched

While the main column waits in a shallow depression, Custer & *C Troop* join the scouts.

Reno halts when fighting starts

Reno deploys into battle formation

Upland Ridge

Deep Coulee

East Ridge

Medicine Tail Coulee

Cedar Coulee

The Peak

N

200 Yards

The Timber

The Bluffs

Crow scouts

F Troop detail

Custer

Half Yellow Face

The Flat

Reno

Little Big Horn R.

As far as can be determined, the order of march as Custer crossed North Fork Creek had the headquarters detachment in the lead, followed by *Troops F, E, C, I,* and *L*. The column forded the narrow creek, moving at a steady trot; but scarcely had a minute passed when things began to go wrong. Members of the headquarters detachment noticed the two Crow scouts were veering too far to the left, heading again toward the southern end of the bluff rather than along its higher elevation. Too far off to stop them, Custer and the rest watched in frustration as Half Yellow Face and his companion passed over the distant rise and out of sight toward Reno.

Custer gave a sharp look at Boyer and repeated his order. The interpreter, who was now *de facto* leader of the remaining scouts, turned to those four men — Curley, Goes Ahead, White Man Runs Him, and Hairy Moccasin — and said: *"Come on! We will go up on the hill and look over."*

Once again, though, there was a misunderstanding. The scouts moved off straight ahead, toward the very summit where the *F Troop* patrol was positioned. Custer, seeing the error, responded immediately. According to Hairy Moccasin, *"Custer was ahead of his command, a short distance behind us. Custer yelled at us to stop, then told us to go to the high hill ahead."*

Boyer finally grasped what the general wanted, and all five riders started toward the edge of the Heights at a gallop. Curley stated that when they got to the top of the rise they *"could see nothing of the village,"* so they continued north. Custer followed at a distance below them, along a roughly parallel course. The acting orderly of *C Troop*, Sgt. Daniel Kanipe, recalled the column turned *"square right"* after traveling about a third of a mile, and Custer *"never left the companies or halted."*

They moved along that course for only a few score yards before turning north again. It was about that time Cooke caught up with the battalion, bringing word the Indians now seemed bent on fighting, though, oddly enough, they were still keeping their distance from the troops.

Moving ahead, the scouts were puzzled by the absence of noteworthy activity in the valley below. There was no sign of Reno's force, nor for that matter was there any indication of the evacuation they had expected to see. By the time they arrived on High Hill, the dust cloud was well to the north, its origins obscured by the still loftier sections of the Bluffs in front of them. It was there they stopped and signaled the general, whose column was entering an extended, shallow depres-

sion situated a mile from the north fork. There Custer gave the order for another halt. Leaving Lt. Cooke in charge of the headquarters detachment, he — together with trumpeter John Martin, his nephew Autie Reed, and the whole of Capt. Tom Custer's *C* (*Light Horse*) *Troop* — moved out of line and began the ascent toward the scouts, arriving about 3:05.

Though Capt. Custer joined his brother at the crest, *C Troop* itself remained just below and to the northeast. *"The general took me with him and we rode to the top of the hill where we could see the village in the valley on the other side of the river,"* recalled Martin. *"It was a large village, but we couldn't see all of it from there, though we didn't know it then."*

Custer was visibly relieved by what he did see. He began to realize the Indians were not moving at all nor, apparently, had they been forewarned of his presence. He may have achieved that rarest of military successes: complete operational and tactical surprise. More significant, though, was the fact the warriors then beginning to stall Reno were only a comparative handful. Custer instinctively assumed that, with all the warriors of the encampment busy with Reno, he would

Hairy Moccasin
Scout attached to 7TH CAVALRY

be able to sweep down, enter the village and round up the ponies — which certainly must be close at hand — thereby entirely immobilizing the enemy. Thus, in a single, daring stroke he would gain a spectacular victory that would end what already was being called the "Great Sioux War." Reporter Kellogg would be there to witness the triumph first hand.

The hill, however, did not provide the complete visual perspective Custer had hoped. He could see the valley well enough, but the tree-lined banks of the river, and the awkward angle of the heights themselves, hid most of the tepees. So he decided to move farther north, toward the High Bluffs, which would afford him a better view.

The general spurred his horse, the rest following close behind. When the four men arrived atop the first knoll — the spot also occupied by the *F Troop* patrol — there was still no sign of any large number of hostiles. There for the first time it became clear the dust cloud had been thrown up by a vast herd of running ponies that were being driven down the valley. Indeed, there was a second, equally large mass of ponies several miles to the northwest. Directly ahead, in the valley below, was an astonishing array of lodges, hundreds and hundreds of them, arrayed in a pattern a mile wide and more than twice as long.

It was far larger than anything Custer had anticipated, but there was still little visible activity by any inhabitants other than women and children. As Martin related: "*The general seemed both surprised and glad, and said the Indians must all be in their tepees asleep. We didn't see anything of Reno's column when we were up on the hill. I am sure the general did not see them at all because he looked with his field glasses, and all he said was that we had* 'got them this time.' *He turned in his saddle and took off his hat and waved it to the men of the command who were waiting at the base of the hill.*"

Custer was jubilant, and the four troops of the main column moved forward. Only *C Troop* remained in place. The general had scanned the area to the north when he came up the knoll, noticing Cedar Coulee led to an even larger natural outlet that almost certainly he must have hoped gave access to the river. He promptly ordered *F Troop* to move down toward it, then set out himself at a rapid gait to just opposite where the coulee began. There he turned about, waiting for the head of the main column to come up onto the summit of the High Bluffs. "*We were charging at full speed,*" said Sgt. Kanipe. "*Reno and his troops were seen to our left, moving down the valley.*"

Far below, Reno's command emerged from the mist of historical obscurity to begin its attack on the village. The attention of those on the Heights then became riveted by the awe-inspiring immensity of Sitting Bull's encampment. Kanipe stated that, at the sight, the troopers "*began to holler and yell.*"

Custer took off his broad brimmed hat again, exuberantly waving it back and forth as the men passed by, a gesture also spotted by some in Reno's battalion. The electrifying feeling of the moment was contagious, and several of the *Light Horse* troopers' mounts reared. Trumpeter Martin recalled: "*Some fast horses wanted to go ahead, and it was hard to hold them back.*"

That was equally true of the animals on the bluff, as Sgt. Kanipe related: "*The men were on the hill and all of them gave three cheers. Riding at full gallop past Gen. Custer, he shouted to them, 'Boys, hold on to your horses; there are plenty of Sioux down there for all of us!'*"

Just as the end of the formation moved into Cedar Coulee, Custer spoke to his brother, and then began to move along the bluff-top at a rapid pace. Tom returned to his company to tell Sgt. Kanipe: "*Go to Capt. McDougall. Tell him to bring the pack train straight across the high ground. If any packs come loose, don't stop to fix them; cut them off and come quick. [There's a] big Indian camp. If you see Capt. Benteen, tell him to come quick.*"

The sergeant turned south while the scouts and *C Troop* again hastened after their leader. Even as they did so, Pvt. McIllhargey rode up with the redundant news that Reno's command had completed its crossing of the river. Kanipe took a final glimpse of what was going on there, noting the general and the rest had come close to the tepees of the nearest Indian circle, which was situated at the very base of the bluffs on the east side of the river. He recalled: "*Custer and his troops were within half-a-mile of the Indian camp,*" though they were still far above it. Looking to his right he could also "*see Reno and his three companies and about 35 Indian scouts going right toward the Indian camp.*"

That was, undoubtedly, one of the last moments before the actual fighting began in the valley below. Reno's command was charging toward the village as his scouts were moving left to capture the many straggling Indian ponies. Kanipe himself then rode to carry out his orders. In the meantime, sending the *Light Horse Troop* forward some 500 yards, the general allowed the Crow scouts to catch up with him. Remembered Goes Ahead: "*Custer rode to the very edge of the High Bluffs and looked over to the place where Reno's men were, as though planning his next move.*"

Though Reno's charge already was slowing down, with more and more Indians firing at them, Custer did not stay to observe the outcome. Turning toward his companions he said: *"We will go down and make a crossing and capture the village."*

Pausing, he again spoke to Mitch Boyer. According to Hairy Moccasin, *"Custer told us to go to the top of the hill ahead* [the Peak]. *From there we could see the valley and see the Reno fight."*

The general then rode back to rejoin *C Troop*, exclaiming: *"Custer's Luck, boys! We've caught them napping! We'll finish them off then go back to our station! Come on!"* The men raised another cheer, then all spurred their mounts and descended the slope to rejoin their comrades in the main column, which had halted midway along Cedar Coulee.

By this time the *F Troop* detail had arrived at its objective on the rise directly above the juncture with Medicine Tail Coulee. Reno's command had started to lay down a heavy fire at 3:18 p.m., thus initiating the opening round of what would turn into the Battle of the Little Bighorn. Simultaneously, Custer stationed his brother's troop at the head of the column. He then rejoined his staff, telling Cooke what he had seen, and led the battalion forward. The new order of march was: headquarters detachment, *C, F, E, I,* and *L Troops*.

In the meantime, Boyer and the other scouts reached the top of the Peak. *"When Custer left,"* said Curley, *"Mitch and we scouts remained on the point. When we looked down at the camp we noticed there were not many Indians around, and Mitch said he thought they were somewhere else, and suggested we go down."*

They just saw the opening round of the Reno fight before departing; for by then Custer was already on his way. His column entered the Medicine Tail at 3:21. rejoined shortly by the *F Troop* patrol.

The battalion halted soon after entering Medicine Tail Coulee. Custer summoned Trumpeter Martin.

[Gen. Custer] was about 200 yards from his command. I could see the Indian village but not Maj. Reno's command. The general said to me, 'Orderly, I want you to take a message to Benteen. Ride as fast as you can and tell him to be quick, and to bring the packs!' He didn't stop at all when he was telling me this, and I just said 'Yes Sir!' and kicked my horse when the adjutant said, 'Wait, Orderly, I'll give you a message!' And he stopped and wrote it in a big hurry in a little black notebook, and then tore out the leaf and gave it to me.

Martin took the paper and, after tucking it into his shirt pocket, headed south: *"My horse was pretty tired, but I started back as fast as I could go. The last I saw of the command, they were going down into the ravine. The Gray Horse Troop was in the center, and they were galloping."*

Boyer's party caught up to the headquarters detachment just after the column came to a halt. Said Hairy Moccasin: *"We scouts turned* [from the Peak] *and charged north to where Custer was headed."* According to Curley, the general *"finally came out at Medicine Tail Coulee and, seeing he was very far from the valley, Custer turned left and went down the coulee."* The scout and his companions followed, noting: *"After a while he halted the command."*

Custer had stopped because he saw the first evidence of hostiles directly ahead of him. He was less than two miles from the river. The scouts had barely caught up when the headquarters detachment began moving again. Hairy Moccasin said: *"When we met Custer he asked, 'How is it?' I said 'Reno's men are fighting hard!'"* It was 3:23 p.m.

Though Custer was entering the fight under the impression the majority of the Indians were indisposed, he had good reason to suspect the 10 or so braves to his front, as well as those challenging Reno in the valley, were part of the much larger group seen an hour earlier on the bluffs he had just traversed. Though tactical surprise had been achieved and the initiative was in his hands, he was not about to rush ahead blindly.

At the moment there was only token opposition, but that would soon change. Unknown to Custer there were more than 3,600 warriors in and around the village, which was double the number the general had been told he could expect to find. He had, however, been essentially correct in his assessment the hostiles had been "caught napping." Now they were wide awake, though, with most of them drawn toward the smaller, but much closer, threat posed by Reno. Custer was soon to discover his own force was facing upward of 150 warriors. Scarcely had trumpeter Martin begun to make his way toward the High Bluffs when things began to unravel: *"I heard firing [in] back of me and I looked around and saw Indians, some waving buffalo robes and some shooting. They had been in ambush."*

Two parties, each of five Sioux, had suddenly materialized without warning: the first from a shallow de-

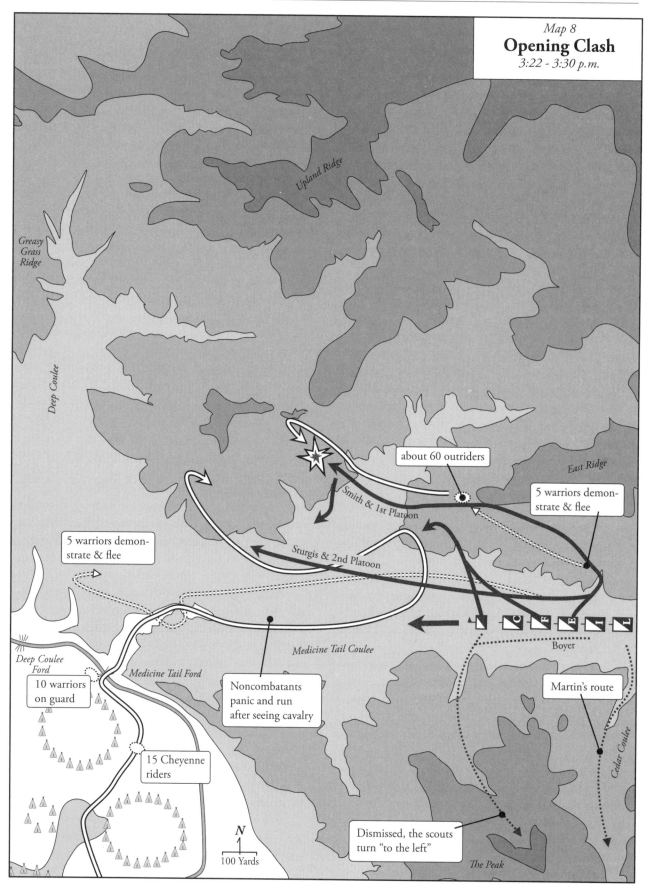

Map 8
Opening Clash
3:22 - 3:30 p.m.

Upland Ridge

Greasy Grass Ridge

Deep Coulee

East Ridge

about 60 outriders

5 warriors demonstrate & flee

Smith & 1st Platoon

5 warriors demonstrate & flee

Sturgis & 2nd Platoon

A C F E I L

Boyer

Medicine Tail Coulee

Deep Coulee Ford

10 warriors on guard

Medicine Tail Ford

Martin's route

15 Cheyenne riders

Noncombatants panic and run after seeing cavalry

Cedar Coulee

Dismissed, the scouts turn "to the left"

The Peak

N

100 Yards

pression in the coulee — shooting, war-whooping and waving their robes — while the second group emerged from behind a cluster of cherry bushes on the slopes of East Ridge to the right. They all fired their weapons into the air in an unsuccessful attempt to spook the soldiers' horses. Custer spurred out of line and, according to Curley, *"rode to an officer who seemed to be in command of one of the troops, which had gray horses, and gave an order. Immediately the troops turned toward the Little Bighorn."*

The *Gray Horse (E) Troop* moved toward its right and started down the creek crossing Medicine Tail Coulee, then went straight toward the Indians on the ridge, who in turn quickly headed off toward the northwest, trying to link up with a sizable body of other patrolling Indian outriders. *E Troop* split into two sections. The unit's senior officer, Lt. Algernon Smith, moved directly ahead with *1st Platoon*, while Lt. J.C. Sturgis led the *2nd* off to the left, down the coulee. On seeing that, the braves in front of Custer's column likewise began to flee in the direction of the river, even as their counterparts on East Ridge joined the outrider group and together took off toward the next ridge line.

As the two platoons pursued their respective quarry, the general returned to the head of the still moving main column and ordered a halt. Turning to Boyer he said: *"You scouts need go no farther. You are not to fight in this battle. Go back and save your lives. You have led me here and your work is finished; so you had better go back to the pack train and let the soldiers do the fighting."*

Then, after directing *F Troop* to come forward and the main column to remain in place, Custer led off the headquarters detachment at a vigorous trot. As he did so, the three remaining troops — *C, I,* and *L* — closed up while the interpreter relayed his new instructions to the other Crow. At first confused and shocked by their dismissal, they soon recovered and followed in Custer's wake. The general did not go far, though, just a few hundred yards. *"Here the column halted again,"* remembered Curley. *"Custer wrote a message and handed it to a young man on a sorrel horse who galloped away."*

Having observed *E Troop's* actions, Custer led the headquarters detachment and *F Troop* at full gallop toward East Ridge. The scouts, again left behind, moved down the coulee a short distance. *"Mitch Boyer decided to return to the Bluffs,"* said Goes Ahead. The scouts *"turned to the left along the ridge overlooking the river, while Custer led his command to the right."*

Meanwhile the main column, with Myles Keogh in charge, received the general's message and moved

ahead for a time. As the Crow continued their ascent, the three troops did not stop until they were within a mile of Medicine Tail Ford, while off to the north Custer and his men arrived on East Ridge. From there Custer had an unobstructed view down to the river and a panoramic sweep of the coulee as it branched off into a broad, fork-like expanse framed by low ridges. He saw Lt. Smith's platoon had galloped to the northwest to the base of Upland Ridge to open fire on the outriders, who then numbered about 60 warriors.

That was the first clash between the Custer battalion and its opposition. The Indians held on to the high ground, and in the following three minutes Smith, in the face of strengthening opposition, shifted about 200 yards to the left. Without dismounting, *1st Platoon* began pushing uphill at a trot, driving the warriors back to a point just over the crest of the ridge, but there Smith chose not go any farther.

Simultaneously, Lt. Sturgis had been chasing his five Sioux, whose fresher, faster ponies carried them farther and farther away. Suddenly 15 Cheyenne came hurtling up the Medicine Tail. The smaller group of combatants passed them near East Ridge, continuing down the coulee, then turning north while the Cheyenne wheeled left, letting go a burst of gunfire. Sturgis went after the new opponents, following them until he reached a point about a quarter-mile west of *1st Platoon*. There he halted for a time, still shooting at the fading enemy, then moved again toward the Little Bighorn at full speed, slowing down only after coming to within 150 yards of Medicine Tail Ford at 3:33 p.m.

Prior to Sturgis' arrival at the ford, the approach of Custer's battalion had gone almost unnoticed by those in Sitting Bull's encampment. It was not until a large mob of women and children — who only moments before had crossed the river seeking safe haven — erupted in screams of terror, that the warriors in the camp became aware of the new force of bluecoats. As the noncombatants hot-footed it back down Medicine Tail Coulee, a brave named Bobtail Horse was the first to actually see the second column, then less than two miles east of the Non-Agency Cheyenne circle.

Shouting the alarm the instant before a fresh rattle of gunfire was heard, Bobtail Horse and three others had a clear view of the entire length of the coulee. Initially there seemed to be only indecipherable confusion and swirling dust, but when they were at last able to make out the battalion's formation, an Indian named White Shield saw it had divided into seven segments.

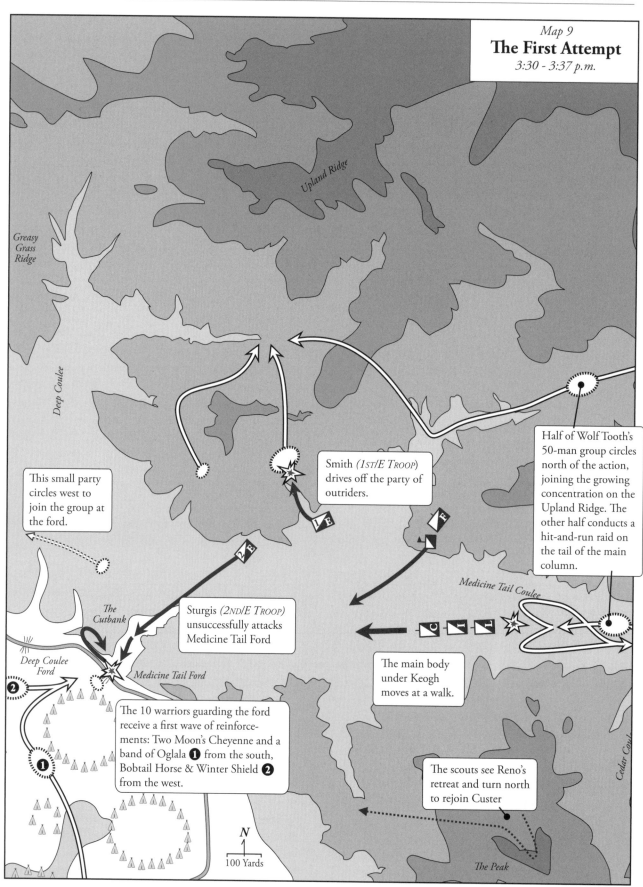

Map 9
The First Attempt
3:30 - 3:37 p.m.

Upland Ridge

Greasy Grass Ridge

Deep Coulee

Smith *(1ST/E TROOP)* drives off the party of outriders.

Half of Wolf Tooth's 50-man group circles north of the action, joining the growing concentration on the Upland Ridge. The other half conducts a hit-and-run raid on the tail of the main column.

This small party circles west to join the group at the ford.

Medicine Tail Coulee

The Cutbank

Sturgis *(2ND/E TROOP)* unsuccessfully attacks Medicine Tail Ford

Deep Coulee Ford

Medicine Tail Ford

The main body under Keogh moves at a walk.

The 10 warriors guarding the ford receive a first wave of reinforcements: Two Moon's Cheyenne and a band of Oglala ❶ from the south, Bobtail Horse & Winter Shield ❷ from the west.

The scouts see Reno's retreat and turn north to rejoin Custer

Cedar Coulee

N
100 Yards

The Peak

Doubtless he saw the division of *E Troop* into two platoons, the headquarters detachment and *F Troop* atop East Ridge, and the main column (*C, I,* and *L Troops*) on the move.

The braves were uncertain exactly what the soldiers were going to do, so they did not move until *2nd Platoon* drew close to the ford. White Shield noted the *"five Sioux who were running gradually veered away from a part of the soldiers, and the troops did not follow them but kept [moving] toward the river."*

Bobtail Horse, together with his friends — Calf, Roan Bear, and Joseph White Cow Bull — rode single file from the circle toward the ford at 3:30, soon followed by White Shield, who was in turn joined by a veteran named Mad Wolf. Of the six, all but one was Cheyenne. Those young men, together with others already stationed at the ford, raised to 16 the total of warriors there to challenge Lt. Sturgis and his 18-man platoon. As the warriors rushed toward the ford, the troops, though moving at a rapid gait, were still off a fair distance. Mad Wolf counseled the others: *"No one must charge on the soldiers; there are too many!"*

One glance at the formidable array of bluecoats extending up the coulee confirmed the wisdom of his advice. They could see such tactics would have no chance of success. *"It's no use,"* said one, *"we can't stop them!"*

They went forward anyway, determined to do what they could in defense of their village, however futile, whatever the cost. They were the first reinforcements to reach Medicine Tail. White Shield and Mad Wolf felt the crossing point was already becoming overcrowded, and the soldiers were much too close; so they turned left to go behind a low berm to the north. As they and the Bobtail Horse group reached the river and dismounted, the hard-riding platoon of *Gray Horse* troopers inexplicably stopped short of it (this was Sturgis' second short halt 150 yards shy of the ford).

All became dead silent near the ford; there was suddenly no sound or disturbance of any kind. The soldiers stayed on their horses; those in the lead carefully scrutinizing the area ahead. Their caution may have reflected the fact Lt. Sturgis was one of the regiment's least experienced officers, even though he was being assisted by the company's more knowledgeable First Sergeant, Frederick Hohemeyer.

Bobtail Horse and the rest of the braves were hunkered down behind a berm close to the river, watching and waiting. Directly before them was a passage two-to-five feet deep across a stream 30 yards wide. Carpeting the river bed was a layer of slippery pebbles and stones. Except for the well-worn exit paths, the soft earthen banks remained steep and untouched.

Sturgis seemed genuinely amazed by the sudden tranquility he beheld, and so he again led forward his column. The platoon advanced two abreast at a steady pace to the water's edge, but instead of just charging across the lieutenant hesitated again. He intently studied the other bank in a final scan, then turned his gaze down at the stream itself, studying its depth. As he did so, three Oglala came riding up from the west. They jumped off their ponies and began to fire at the soldiers even before reaching cover. Those who originally had been on guard at the ford joined in. *"The 10 were firing as hard as they could,"* recalled Bobtail Horse.

The startled officer shouted an order to his men, then all moved out at a fast gait. They plunged into the river despite the fusillade of arrows and bullets, but got no farther than mid-stream before they began to fall. First to go down was Hohemeyer, then Sturgis, then the guidon bearer. The others pulled up quickly. A few jumped from their horses into the water, gathered the fallen, then carried them back to the east side.

With all the splashing and gun smoke and milling about, it was difficult for the tribesmen to make out what was happening. One thing was certain: the cavalry advance had been stopped. The defenders had done what they thought was impossible, and they watched with relief as the blue-clad formation reversed course.

The troopers redeployed themselves behind the riverbank. As they did so the Indians discovered something else about them, their physical condition. *"When the soldiers attacked they were clearly exhausted,"* remembered Sitting Bull, *"but they began to fight at once, but by then our camps were aroused and there were plenty of warriors to meet them."*

The platoon had clearly been struck a paralyzing blow, having been left leaderless. It appears a brief stalemate ensued. The soldiers remained in place, weapons blazing, even as more Indians began to arrive.

Up to that moment almost all the braves in the village, from Sitting Bull down, had been focused on meeting the threat at the village's upper end (Reno's battalion). While moving in that direction, a few had caught a lucky glimpse of the Custer battalion as it moved along the High Bluffs. Among them was the Hunkpapa war chief, Gall. He was a respected warrior and leader of the host tribal band in the valley; as such he had *de jure* authority over the confederation of Sioux and Cheyenne. That control, never absolute, re-

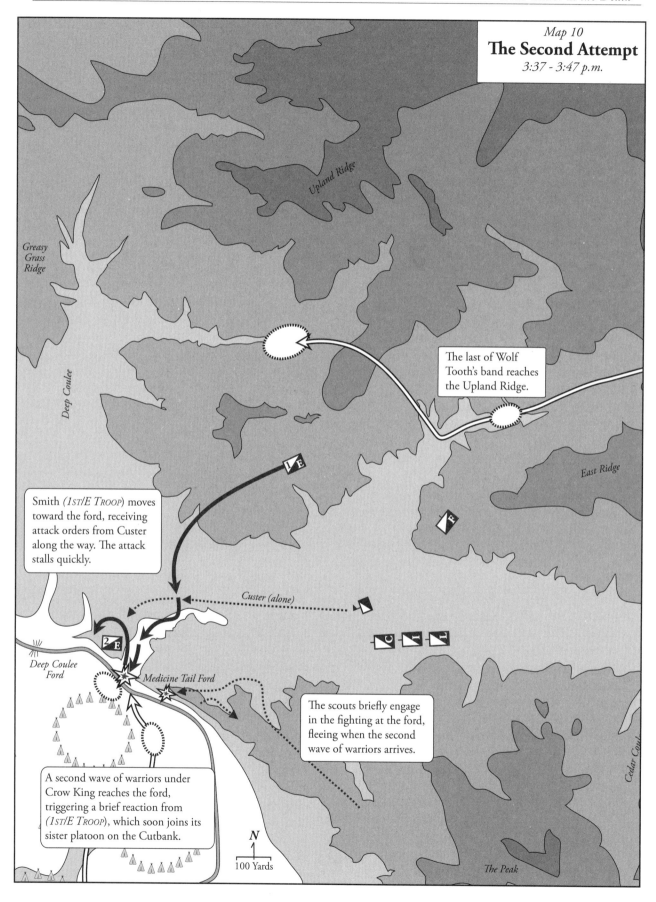

Map 10
The Second Attempt
3:37 - 3:47 p.m.

Upland Ridge

Greasy Grass Ridge

Deep Coulee

The last of Wolf Tooth's band reaches the Upland Ridge.

East Ridge

1/E

F

Smith *(1st/E Troop)* moves toward the ford, receiving attack orders from Custer along the way. The attack stalls quickly.

Custer (alone)

C I L

2/E

Deep Coulee Ford

Medicine Tail Ford

The scouts briefly engage in the fighting at the ford, fleeing when the second wave of warriors arrives.

A second wave of warriors under Crow King reaches the ford, triggering a brief reaction from *(1st/E Troop)*, which soon joins its sister platoon on the Cutbank.

Cedar Coulee

N

100 Yards

The Peak

ally amounted to deferential rather than unquestioned power. Thus he later would remark with a good degree of truth: *"I can't say I or anyone else was in command."*

Gall himself had been off to the west just prior to Reno's attack, and had been one of those who spotted Custer on the Heights. Instantly perceiving the new danger, he moved toward the village proper. Once there, he encountered the last groups preparing to move against Reno, and began redirecting them toward Medicine Tail Ford. He did not go there himself until the battle was well underway, so the tactical leader of the first large warrior influx was the Non-Agency Cheyenne war chief Two Moon.

The 161-man contingent of Cheyenne, Arapahoe and Gros Ventres following Two Moon were only the first of a growing build-up of Indians in the Medicine Tail area. The warriors did not turn against "Long Hair" *en masse*, or in a steady flow, but rather as segmented bodies of affiliated bands. They came on in what might be best described as a series of tribal waves. The process took place gradually, at intervals of alternating lengths that seem to have been determined primarily by the diminishing threat posed by Reno. It therefore took a while for the Indians to respond with anything approaching their full weight of numbers. Once Custer's presence became known, though, *"word passed among the Indians like a whirlwind,"* recalled Red Horse.

As the leading elements of the Non-Agency Cheyenne moved north along the western edge of the village, then right, past the Blackfoot and Sans Arc circles, they became alarmed when they found Custer's troops had already reached the river. Guided by a sub-chief, Yellow Nose, the Cheyenne began firing as they advanced. There was a commotion among the soldiers, who then let loose a solid volley in return.

As more hostiles rode in and began crowding the riverbank, the leaderless men of *2ND PLATOON* realized they had only one option remaining. At 3:37 they retreated to their right, to the Cutbank overlooking the Little Bighorn. From there they were still able to lay down fire on the ford.

Though Custer had suffered a setback, he was probably not even aware of it at that moment since there were other problems occupying his attention. At the same time the advance across Medicine Tail Ford was stalled, the rear of the main column was struck by a mixed band of some 50 warriors under the leadership of a Cheyenne named Wolf Tooth. He had moved in from the east, coming rapidly down the coulee. Keogh's

column had been advancing and temporarily dropped from view, with the result Wolf Tooth's band split in two parts. Some followed the soldiers while the rest went around the eastern end of East Ridge in anticipation of striking them from the right flank. The first group managed to catch up with the tail end of *L TROOP* and launched a hit-and-run raid on both sides of it. They then headed back the way they had come and reunited with their comrades while the soldiers continued toward the river.

Even the Crow scouts, who meanwhile had arrived on the High Bluffs, noticed a significant increase in activity. *"Everybody around us was shooting,"* said White Man Runs Him, *"and no one could tell the place where the firing was [being] done."*

For Custer, from his vantage on East Ridge, the unexpected harassment seemed a troublesome but still minor annoyance. Using his field glasses to watch the actions of both *E TROOP* platoons, it must have seemed clear to him *1ST PLATOON*, on the right, had matters in hand. The skirmish line there was holding the slopes of Upland Ridge against the party of Indian outriders, who, in spite of their numerical advantage, had begun to move off to the northeast. On reaching the next ridge line a quarter-mile away, they were joined by Wolf Tooth and his following, which brought their total strength to upward of 130.

Leaving *F TROOP* on East Ridge, the headquarters detachment signaled the main column at 3:35, then they all began traveling toward the river and continued that way until the troops already at the ford began their withdrawal. Interestingly, Pvt. Mitchell, the last of the couriers from Reno, had only just arrived with word of the major's advance down the valley. Custer thereupon decided to ride ahead for a personal "looksee," by which time he felt confident enough about the safety of his right flank to order *1ST PLATOON* to move farther west.

In the meantime, trumpeter Martin was having difficulty retracing his steps along Cedar Coulee as he had been ordered to do, since his horse had become thoroughly fatigued. While still en route he met the general's younger brother, a civilian who had been left with the pack train: *"Just before I got to the top of the hill I met Boston Custer. He asked me, 'Where's the general?' I answered, 'Right around the next ridge.'"*

That exchange took place about 3:32. Martin stated he warned the young man about the Indians, then the two separated. A minute later the orderly was back atop the High Bluffs. He recalled, *"When I got to the*

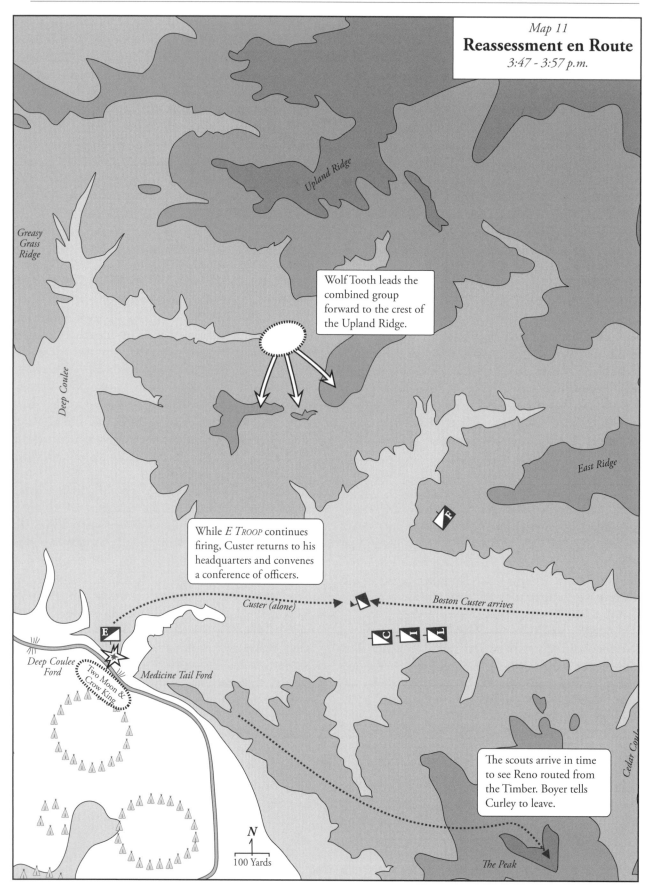

Map 11
Reassessment en Route
3:47 - 3:57 p.m.

Upland Ridge

Greasy
Grass
Ridge

Wolf Tooth leads the
combined group
forward to the crest of
the Upland Ridge.

Deep Coulee

East Ridge

While *E Troop* continues
firing, Custer returns to his
headquarters and convenes
a conference of officers.

Custer (alone)   Boston Custer arrives

E

Deep Coulee
Ford

Two Moon &
Crow King

Medicine Tail Ford

Cedar Coulee

The scouts arrive in time
to see Reno routed from
the Timber. Boyer tells
Curley to leave.

N

100 Yards

The Peak

top of the hill, I looked down and saw Reno's battalion in action." Just a few minutes earlier he *"had seen no Indians. But [now] there was lots of them, riding around and shooting at Reno's men, who were dismounted and in a skirmish line. I did not have time to stop and watch; I had to get to Benteen, but the last I saw of Reno's men, they were fighting in the valley and the line was falling back."*

In short, Reno already was making his withdrawal to the nearby timber lining the river. Boyer and the Crow scouts had reached the Peak about the same time. They did not specifically mention seeing any retreat at that time, but did infer that it was taking place. They tell of a skirmish line having deployed along the front of the village, and they claimed there were too many Indians, and Reno had in fact already been defeated. They also heard the opening rounds of the fight at Medicine Tail Ford, observing Two Moon's first wave heading in that direction. Then the scouts left the Peak, taking nine minutes to reach Black Butte. They moved behind the elevation to avoid being seen. *"As we followed the high ground,"* said White Man Runs Him, *"Custer had come down the Medicine Tail Coulee and was moving toward the river."*

Martin also saw Custer's move toward the ford. He had pulled up on the knoll from which Custer had first spotted the village. Looking back a last time, *"I saw not only Reno, but Custer as well, and I saw him and his command right down to within a few hundred yards of the river, retreating from it."* Martin then moved on, finally meeting Benteen in the Flat at 3:59.

The movement spotted by Martin and the Crow scouts was Custer and the *1ST PLATOON* of *E TROOP*, not moving together but arriving simultaneously at the draw leading to the crossing. Proceeding down the coulee, Custer arrived at the elevated Cutbank held by *2ND PLATOON* at 3:44. Smith and the *1ST PLATOON* came into line to the left of the Cutbank, where it dismounted to begin clearing the area around the ford to create an opening for the main column.

The calamitous new crash of carbines startled Boyer and his party. Leaving the Peak, Boyer and the Crow scouts entered a narrow ravine wedged into the northeast corner of the Bluffs. Via that circuitous route they made their way to the end of the cliffs just above the ford. Able to see across the tops of the tribal circle lodges into the heart of the village, the dismounted Crow noted there were thousands in the camp.

Then, across the open plain and through the village came the throngs of Sitting Bull's second wave. Led by

the pre-eminent Sioux sub-chief Crow King, they numbered more than 500 warriors from the Hunkpapa, Santee, and Yankton tribes. The Crow scouts gasped at the foreboding sight.

Preceded by the five who originally had been forced out of hiding in the coulee, along with the village elder-warriors, the second wave began arriving at 3:45, bringing the total number facing Custer to nearly 700. *"During this time,"* said Curley, *"the warriors were seen riding out of the valley by the hundreds, deploying across his [Custer's] front to the left [south] as if to cross the stream."*

Alarmed, the general led Smith's platoon forward to try to counter the threat. Even as he did so, one of the horses became unmanageable, carrying his unfortunate rider to the ford where he fell, riddled with bullets. His comrades, however, reined in and dismounted, deploying along the stream itself, shooting as they went. *"I know for sure Custer went right down to the riverbank,"* said White Man Runs Him, *"I saw him go that far. The Sioux were right across the river. Custer fired. That was the first firing Custer did."*

In that way a searing, pointblank exchange erupted along both sides of the Little Bighorn, and again a stalemate developed. After a short time several officers climbed a low bluff to get a better view. Concluding the situation was hopeless, Sturgis and his men withdrew at 3:46. Said White Shield: *"The troops of cavalry that came closest to Bobtail Horse fell back to the side of a little knoll and stopped there."*

It seemed obvious to the Crow scouts not only that all hope of using Medicine Tail Ford was gone, but that the battalion was doomed. Accordingly, they leaped on their horses and hurried back in the direction they had come.

Though they never provided details about their return journey, it appears the scouts moved along the crest of Black Butte, trying to get away from the battle as quickly as possible. Their various narratives pick up again only after they reached the Peak for the third time in less than an hour. It seems Boyer was beginning to have second thoughts about their retreat, and together with Curley he stopped at the top of the elevation while the three other Crow did the same a bit farther on. There they viewed the sorry spectacle of the Reno battalion in full flight from the timber toward the Heights. *"I had seen Reno defeated and discussed it with Mitch,"* remembered Curley.

In an unsuccessful effort to outflank Reno's routing troopers, some Blackfoot and Sans Arc had crossed the

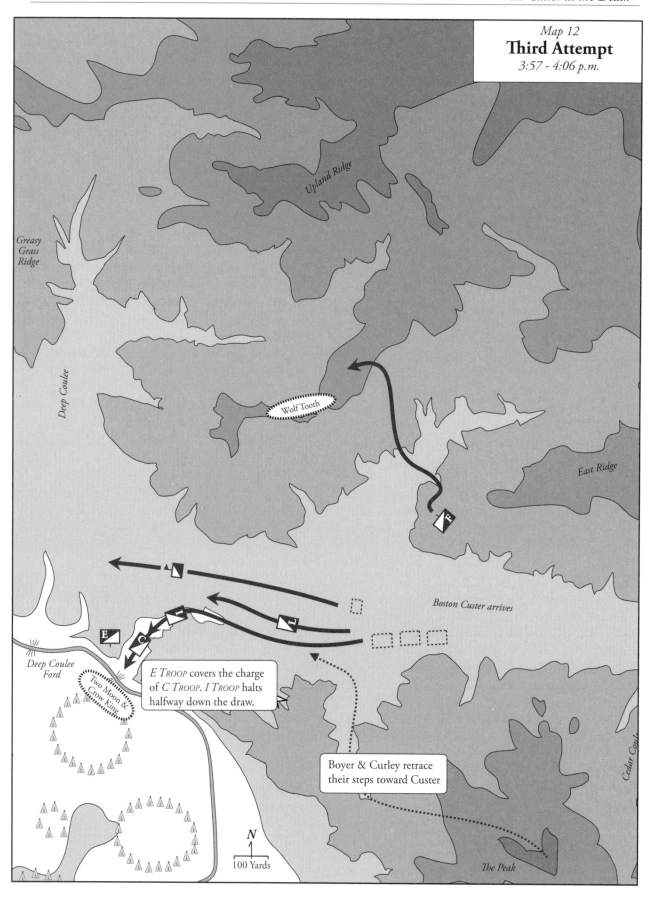

Map 12
Third Attempt
3:57 - 4:06 p.m.

Upland Ridge

Greasy Grass Ridge

Deep Coulee

Wolf Tooth

East Ridge

E

I

Boston Custer arrives

E

C

Deep Coulee Ford

Two Moon & Crow King

E TROOP covers the charge of *C TROOP*. *I TROOP* halts halfway down the draw.

Boyer & Curley retrace their steps toward Custer

N

100 Yards

The Peak

Cedar Coulee

river and were milling about aimlessly at the base of the Bluffs. All the scouts fired shots at the enemy below.

Then Boyer called over to the others: *"You go back! I'm going down [to Custer]!"* His sense of duty, and his feeling the general should be notified of the turn of events in the valley, compelled him to gallop north again. The three scouts loosed a final volley toward the hostiles, then rode south toward the end of the Bluffs, there to link up with Benteen.

Boyer rode in the opposite direction, back toward Medicine Tail Coulee, Curley trailed behind. *"We saw no more of Curley,"* Hairy Moccasin later recalled. *"I don't know where he went."*

While the scouts may have been dismayed by the second repulse at the ford, Custer had not given up. Leaving behind *E Troop* to keep the Indians pinned down, he headed back toward the headquarters detachment. The situation around him was not static. To the northeast the 130 hostiles with Wolf Tooth had reoccupied the crest of Upland Ridge. *F Troop* had made no attempt to prevent that, which may indicate its commander, along with those of the main column, had been signaled to ride to the field headquarters for a conference.

The general rejoined his staff at 3:54, just three minutes after Boston Custer's arrival. The fact the latter had gotten through safely was an encouraging sign Benteen's anticipated route behind the bluff was still open. It also provided Custer with a mental picture of that captain's whereabouts, as well as the location of the pack train. As far as anyone knew, Reno's attack was still underway.

In any case, Custer probably informed his officers of the situation, as well as he knew it, and gave his new plan of action. He ordered the division of the main column into two sections. The first, consisting of *C* and *I Troops*, would be his main striking force. The second, *L Troop*, led by his brother-in-law Lt. James C. Calhoun, would make up the ready reserve. To guard the rear of the assault force, *F Troop* would move against the Indians (Wolf Tooth's) on the southern crest of the Upland Ridge.

At 3:57 p.m., Capt. George W. Yates' *F Troop* crossed the rim of Upland Ridge onto Wolf Tooth's left flank. The advance came to an unplanned halt at 4:00 as the Indians could not be dislodged. Worse, the soldiers were about to be struck on their left flank by a party of some 50 Blackfoot warriors approaching from

their left. That force was made up of some of the Blackfoot warriors from the fight against Reno. This group had ascended the High Bluffs and then moved rapidly northwest trying to get into the fight.

Down in the coulee, the main column started forward at the same time as Yates. The first section broke into a run, while *L Troop* trotted slowly behind, and the headquarters detachment moved at an almost languid walk. The leisurely pace belied the urgency of the moment.

Gall observed that Custer's formation was advancing in an irregular, segmented fashion, divided into two groups. The first extended nearly 400 yards ahead of the second by the time it disappeared from his view below the tops of the lodges. Unable to see what was happening at the river, he nevertheless perceived a degree of hesitancy in the movement of the second section, which was in contrast to the tempo of events until then. As he subsequently noted: *"Whatever Custer's attitude, he did not waver in his advance."*

Up on the Bluffs, Boyer and Curley were taking a parallel line along Black Butte. For a time the elevation near the Medicine Tail Coulee blocked their view, but when they reached a small hill at the head of a ravine, the cavalry column reappeared. *"Custer's column came into sight, galloping right down the coulee toward the river,"* he later remembered. Asked how long it took for the troops to reach the river, he replied: *"No time at all."* Curley noted the column never stopped moving: *"it kept on going."* Boyer vigorously signaled Custer, then rode down the ravine to meet him.

As the first section approached Medicine Tail Draw, its narrowness forced both troops to change into a column of twos. By 4:02 *C Troop* had stopped near the river and opened fire while *I Troop* remained about 300 yards behind. *"Only the front part of the column fired,"* said Curley.

During the ensuing exchange, one soldier with stripes on his arms suddenly galloped downstream, past the ford, across the Little Bighorn into the area opposite the Cutbank. No one followed his suicidal move, and he was quickly brought down.

The clash continued for another four minutes in what must have seemed to the scouts a completely futile effort. Then, suddenly, in Curley's words: *"The Troops turned from the mouth of the coulee — the men in the lead motioning with their hands to go northward — when the companies broke from the main column."* Even before the gun smoke had cleared, the entire first section was gone from the area.

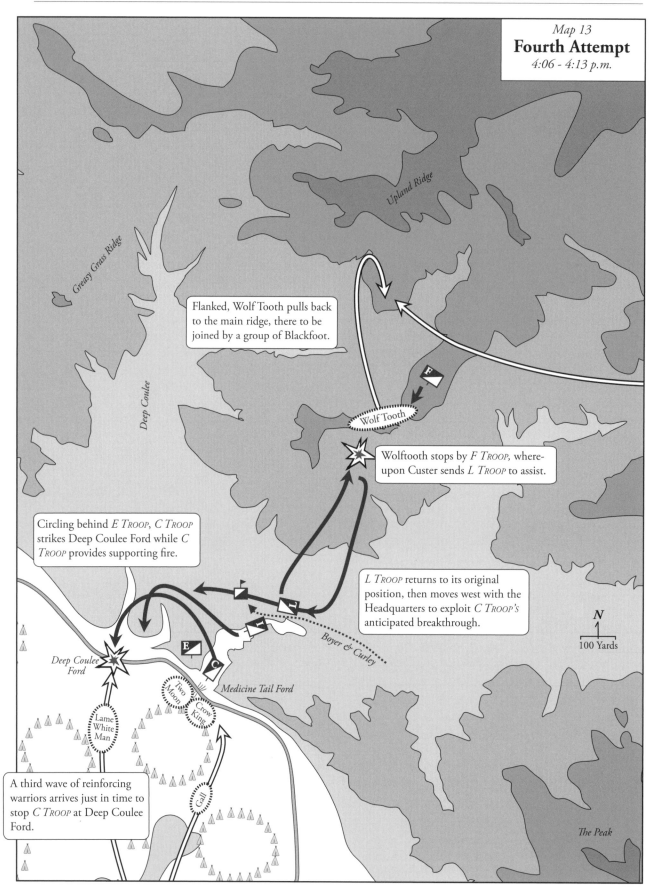

Map 13
Fourth Attempt
4:06 - 4:13 p.m.

Upland Ridge

Greasy Grass Ridge

Deep Coulee

Flanked, Wolf Tooth pulls back to the main ridge, there to be joined by a group of Blackfoot.

Wolf Tooth

Wolftooth stops by *F Troop*, whereupon Custer sends *L Troop* to assist.

Circling behind *E Troop*, *C Troop* strikes Deep Coulee Ford while *C Troop* provides supporting fire.

L Troop returns to its original position, then moves west with the Headquarters to exploit *C Troop's* anticipated breakthrough.

Boyer & Curley

N
100 Yards

Deep Coulee Ford

Medicine Tail Ford

Two Moon

Crow King

Lame White Man

Gall

The Peak

A third wave of reinforcing warriors arrives just in time to stop *C Troop* at Deep Coulee Ford.

The rapid withdrawal was part of Custer's plan. The attack on Medicine Tail Ford had been a feint deliberately undertaken to draw the Indians toward the ford and away from other areas. It had worked, but now that success had to be followed up with an equally daring move downstream.

Meanwhile Boyer and Curley caught up with the headquarters detachment after seven minutes, about three-quarters of a mile from the ford. *"We joined Custer on the Medicine Tail Coulee as he was advancing toward the valley,"* said Curley. *"I saw Mitch saying something to Custer when he met him and [I] presume Mitch must have told him about Reno's situation."*

The news was accepted with equanimity, and though none of them could have known it, during this time Benteen had reached the river at Reno's crossing point (Upper Valley Ford) and then turned north. For his part, the general remained focused on a more pressing concern: the outcome of his revised battle-plan.

The first problem to be dealt with was the new threat to Yates' *F Troop* to the north. Custer dispatched his reserve, Calhoun's *L Troop,* to support Yates. Within three minutes, Wolf Tooth's followers found themselves caught in a crossfire from east and west. That sent the mixed band of braves scrambling for safety to another ridge a half-mile to the northwest. *F Troop* was thereby able to move forward again and secure Upland Ridge's crest. Their success came none too soon: a minute later the Blackfoot group passed over the same spot the soldiers had just vacated. Though the combined strength of the Indians in that area then approached 190, they still were not in any position to harm Yates in his new location.

Calhoun's men returned to their former position just as the second strike of Custer's offensive was about to land. In the hope of supporting a breakthrough into the village, *L Troop* and the headquarters detachment raced another half-mile toward the point of the attack.

C Troop would make this assault as well. Swinging behind *E Troop* on the Cutbank, the *Light Horse* troopers covered a quarter-mile of sloping terrain before arcing toward the mouth of Deep Coulee. Like most of the other hostiles, Two Moon only belatedly

noticed the alarming maneuver: *"I saw flags coming over the hill; to the east the soldiers came all at once, all on horses."*

Once the shift was underway, the general rode on alone toward *E Troop* to observe the outcome of this all-important fourth attack on the ford. Left behind with the still-moving headquarters detachment, Boyer and Curley noted *"Custer himself did not go to the river,"* and that the firing by *Gray Horse (E) Troop* was having its intended effect in keeping the enemy pinned down, unable to cross Medicine Tail Ford. To *E Troop's* right, Myles Keogh's *I Troop* came up to occupy a position along the low escarpment. It appeared to Curley that the cavalrymen would be able charge across the Little Bighorn into the village itself.

It was not be. However, *C Troop* was heading straight into the path of a third wave of mounted hostiles just coming in from the south: more than 200 Agency Cheyenne led by Lame White Man. The air was torn with blood-curdling war cries as the arriving Indians spotted the hated bluecoats. A tremendous burst of small arms fire exploded as the two groups closed on each other. *"The troops did not stop,"* said Curley, *"and some rode into the river."*

That was as far as they got. Running headlong into a storm of gunfire, at least two soldiers were killed immediately. *"The bullets flew so thickly,"* recalled one Sioux warrior, the cavalrymen reeled back. The *Light Horse Troop* put up a strong fight, but even with the support of *I Troop* they were unable to withstand the rapid, close-range deluge. Said Sitting Bull: *"Our young men poured hot lead across the river and drove the whole line back."*

That was the end of Custer's attempts to cross at Medicine Tail Ford. *"After fighting a few minutes,"* said Curley, *"Custer seemed convinced it was impossible to cross. He ordered the column to the right and [they] bore diagonally into the hills downstream."*

The time was 4:13 p.m. At the same moment, Hairy Moccasin and the other Crow scouts met Benteen's battalion, while a minute earlier the last of Reno's men reached the top of the Heights, a hill that one day would bear that officer's name.

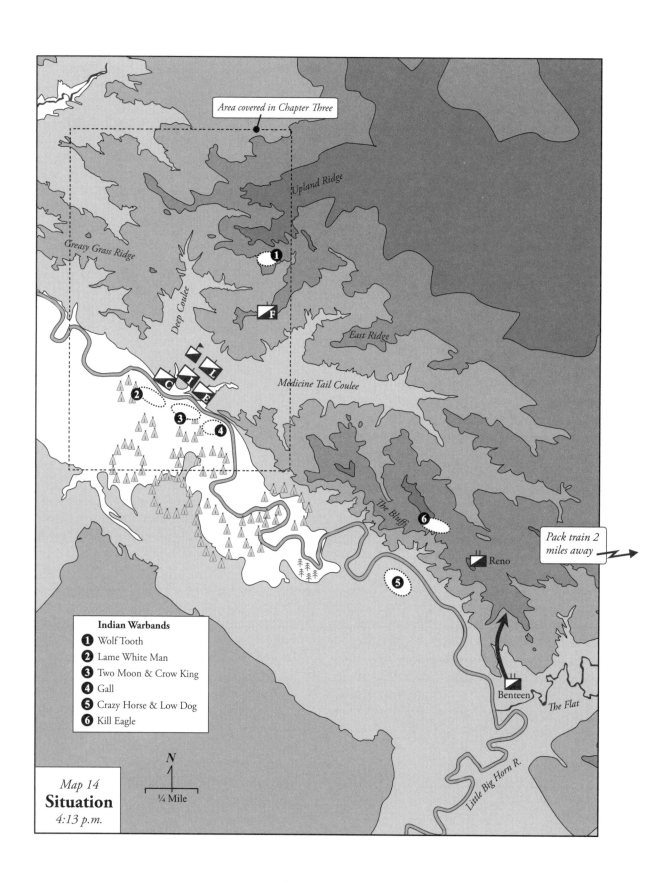

Area covered in Chapter Three

Upland Ridge

Greasy Grass Ridge

Deep Coulee

East Ridge

F

C E
I
L

2

3

4

Medicine Tail Coulee

The Bluffs

6

Pack train 2
miles away

5

Reno

Benteen

The Flat

Little Big Horn R.

Indian Warbands
1 Wolf Tooth
2 Lame White Man
3 Two Moon & Crow King
4 Gall
5 Crazy Horse & Low Dog
6 Kill Eagle

N

¼ Mile

Map 14
Situation
4:13 p.m.

Chapter Three
Greasy Grass Ridge
4:13 p.m. - 5:10 p.m.

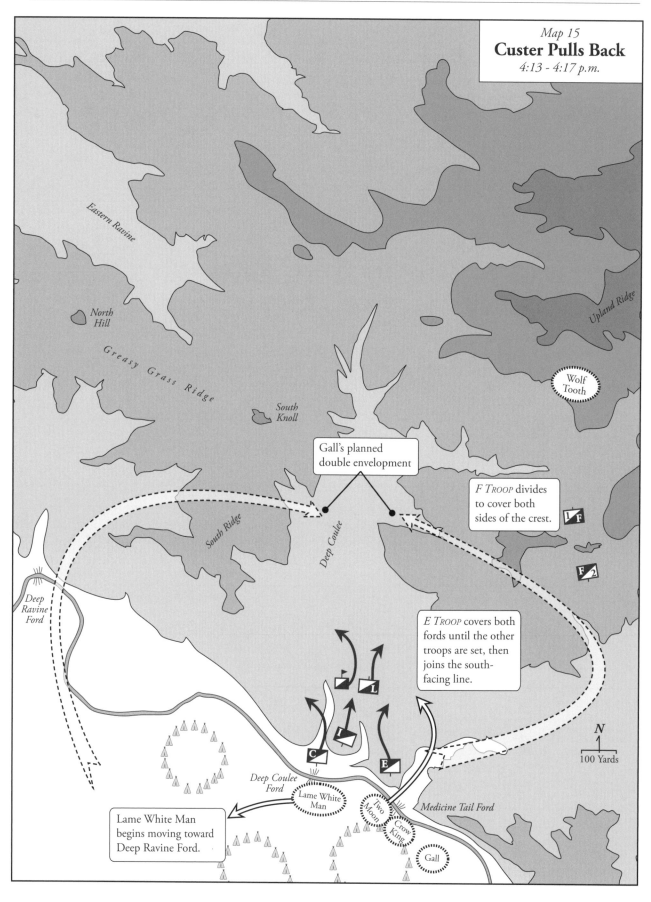

Map 15
Custer Pulls Back
4:13 - 4:17 p.m.

Eastern Ravine

North Hill

Greasy Grass Ridge

South Knoll

Upland Ridge

Wolf Tooth

Gall's planned double envelopment

F TROOP divides to cover both sides of the crest.

1 F

F 2

South Ridge

Deep Coulee

E TROOP covers both fords until the other troops are set, then joins the south-facing line.

Deep Ravine Ford

C

L

L

C

E

N

100 Yards

Deep Coulee Ford

Lame White Man

Two Moon

Crow King

Medicine Tail Ford

Gall

Lame White Man begins moving toward Deep Ravine Ford.

After the repulse at Deep Coulee Ford, Boyer rode forward to talk with the general at the Cutbank overlooking Medicine Tail Ford. On his return he told Curley that *"Custer was seeking a high point [back from the river] to await the arrival of the other troops,"* namely Benteen's battalion and the ammunition-laden pack train. Both had been sent for via couriers nearly an hour before. Having witnessed the defeat of the Reno battalion in the valley, however, Boyer was skeptical; he felt the rest of the *7TH CAVALRY* had *"probably been scared away."*

At the time Custer decided to retreat, he was facing more than 1,100 warriors along the river and some 200 more to his rear. His battalion had taken more than a dozen casualties and was down to about 212 effectives, 95 percent of its original strength.

Since both Medicine Tail Ford and Deep Coulee Crossing had to be kept under continuous fire watch, *E TROOP* once again split into its component platoons for that purpose, thus freeing *C* and *I TROOPS* to withdraw. The pull out began at 4:13, and a new defensive line was established just four minutes later. Said Two Moon: *"They formed three bunches with a little ways [gap] between. Then a bugle sounded and they all got off their horses."*

About a half-mile back from the river, the new line was organized as follows. Tom Custer's *C TROOP* was assigned to defend the extreme western extension of South Ridge; Keogh's *I TROOP* was situated in the Deep Coulee, with *L TROOP* temporarily occupying the lower western slopes of Upland Ridge. The headquarters detachment, under Adjutant Cooke, took up its regulation position about 300 yards to the rear, with one platoon of *F TROOP* on either side of the Upland Ridge.

With his subordinate units repositioned, Custer felt the time had come for all to depart. At about 4:16, *E TROOP*'s two platoons saddled up and rode toward the *L TROOP* position. One platoon replaced it on arrival, while the other shifted right, up the slope, thereby closing the gap between it and *F TROOP* with overlapping fields of fire. As one Cheyenne later confirmed: *"All the soldiers had moved back from the river except the Gray Horse Company, which stood its ground...[then] fell back to the side of a little knoll and stopped there."*

Across the river the leading village war chief, Gall, guided the third wave of more than 400 warriors made up of Agency Cheyenne, Minniconju, and Two Kettle. The Cheyenne, commanded by Lame White Man, arrived on the far north flank, while Gall directed the latter two bands as they came in from the south. He,

like everyone else watching the events at that moment, was under the impression Custer was simply going to withdraw to higher ground. Sizing up the situation in that light, he advised Lame White Man and his own subordinate Hunkpapa sub-chief Crow King to move over the river at Deep Ravine Ford and Medicine Tail, respectively. His basic idea was to create a double-envelopment, while Two Moon, along with Gall himself, would undertake a holding action against the retreating troops.

Even as the new cavalry defense line was being formed, the hostiles began moving across Medicine Tail Ford. *"While Custer was fighting at the Cutbank,"* said Curley, *"I saw no ... Indians ford [the river], but as soon as we began to retreat they must have swarmed across."*

First across was Two Moon leading the Non-Agency Cheyenne, Arapahoe and Gros Ventres; then came Crow King with the Yankton, Santee, and about half the Hunkpapa. Gall, with the Minniconju, Two Kettle, and the remaining Hunkpapa, made up the final contingent. The hostiles grouped into a massive torrent of warriors who poured across the Little Bighorn River *"without discipline,"* recalled one Sioux warrior, *"like bees swarming out of a hive."* To White Shield it seemed the *"Indians were crossing the river and streaming up the gullies like water rushing out of a hose."*

Two Moon led his spearhead group through the splashing water and up the narrow coulee draw, then turned toward Custer's still-forming battle line. Many of the Non-Agency Cheyenne misinterpreted *E TROOP*'s actions, among them Bobtail Horse, who shouted in exultation: *"Come on! They're running! Hurry!"*

He and his comrades leapt onto their ponies and eagerly took after the enemy, followed by many others. Up they surged toward the knoll, but much to their surprise they found the soldiers had turned about. Carbine fire erupted and the Indians recoiled.

Farther downstream (west), Lame White Man turned away from Deep Coulee Crossing in favor of another at the mouth of Deep Ravine. Seeing that, Custer, before rejoining his staff at 4:20, ordered *L TROOP* to the top of South Ridge to counter the Indian move. At that same moment Capt. Frederick Benteen was arriving at High Hill, three miles to the south. On the summit he found, to his dismay, the badly-shaken members of Reno's battalion, just beginning to recover from its rout.

Back at Medicine Tail Ford, Gall's mob, following their Cheyenne allies, were as surprised as Two Moon

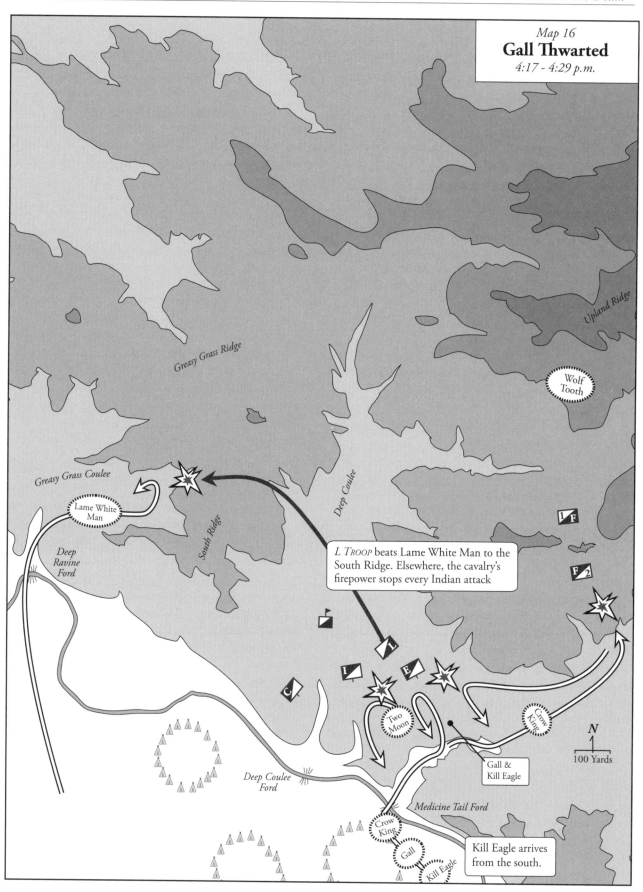

Map 16
Gall Thwarted
4:17 - 4:29 p.m.

Upland Ridge

Greasy Grass Ridge

Wolf
Tooth

Greasy Grass Coulee

Deep Coulee

Lame White
Man

South Ridge

Deep
Ravine
Ford

1 F

F 2

L TROOP beats Lame White Man to the
South Ridge. Elsewhere, the cavalry's
firepower stops every Indian attack

L

I

E

C

Two
Moon

Crow
King

N

100 Yards

Gall &
Kill Eagle

*Deep Coulee
Ford*

Medicine Tail Ford

Crow
King

Gall

Kill Eagle arrives
from the south.

Kill Eagle

by the cavalry's sudden halt. Charging up the ridge to Two Moon's right, they too were met head-on by a hard-shooting defense, the sound of which one of them likened to *"a hail storm before the wind."*

The Indians' euphoria evaporated, and Gall's party wheeled back in haste. Meanwhile Crow King moved straight up Medicine Tail Coulee for about a mile in an effort to effect the planned double-envelopment. He and his Hunkpapa ran into equally formidable resistance from *F Troop's 2nd Platoon*, and were forced to abandon their attempt to ascend Upland Ridge. Moving west, they probed for weakness, a vulnerable spot, only to find themselves blocked by the enemy's overlapping firepower. After a few uncoordinated and ineffectual stabs against Custer's rampart, they fell back beyond Medicine Tail draw to regroup. There they were joined by a fourth wave of reinforcements, Kill Eagle's Blackfoot and Sans Arc who had been fighting Reno. This brought the total Indian strength in the Medicine Tail Coulee to 1,600.

A mile to the northwest, Lame White Man's Agency Cheyenne had fared a little better. *"In the meantime,"* said Curley, *"the Indians had crossed the river below [downstream]…and began to appear on his [Custer's] right and rear."*

Only the timely arrival of *L Troop* atop South Ridge created a vicious and unexpected setback for the hostiles, forcing them to break off their attack, dismount and take cover in Greasy Grass Coulee. The time was 4:29 p.m.

Custer could see that the new position was only a temporary expedient, and that he would have to seek a more tenable one. So, with the immediate threat repulsed, he undertook a full-scale withdrawal toward Greasy Grass Ridge. The battalion began a dismounted retreat in echelon (a V-shaped formation). *C Troop*, to the left of the line, pulled out at 4:30, followed a minute later by *E Troop*, while *I Troop* remained in place until 4:33 to cover the withdrawal.

As the units moved north, they were able to maintain an orderly formation as the men rushed toward the South Knoll of the Greasy Grass, three-quarters of a mile off. Then the still-mounted headquarters detachment *"started out for high ground in a column of fours,"* recalled Curley, *"going directly to the southeast part of the battlefield."* They rode at a full trot, arriving at the hill at 4:34, preceded by the *1st Platoon* of *L Troop*.

The *F Troop* platoons atop Upland Ridge also began a retrograde move. In the most complex maneuver

undertaken in the fight thus far, Custer was trying to achieve a uniform contraction of the battlefront, which then extended in an arc more than a mile in length.

The hostiles were caught off guard by the retreat, and were unable to move immediately against the bluecoats. Then, with Gall in the center, Two Moon to the left and Crow King on the right, the massed warriors once again galloped across the coulees. By the time they closed in, the enemy was nearly halfway to their goal. Whereas the withdrawal from the river to the first line of defense had been hurried, this second shift was methodical. *"They kept pretty good order,"* remembered Sitting Bull.

At no time did the soldiers stop or pause during their move toward the base of South Knoll. As the Minniconju sub-chief Hump recalled: *"They retreated slowly; but it was no time at all before the Indians had Long Hair and his men surrounded."*

The harassment became relentless. Sorely pressed, the men held their mounts by the bridle while fending off their fearless, terrifying foes. It was Keogh's troopers who bore the brunt of the new Indian efforts. Since they were the rearguard, moving about 150 yards behind *C* and *E Troops*, that could only have been expected; at least two more men were lost. Custer himself may also have been with them, sharing their danger, since Mitch Boyer — ever present at the general's side — had his horse shot from under him and was also wounded during this action. *"Coming up from the river [with] Sioux on all sides, except [the] front…"* said Curley, *"they were thrusting on our right and left flanks, firing into us heavily. I don't know how the command made it without some [significant] loss."*

The Indians continued their attacks for as long as possible, but by 4:38 the convergence of four cavalry companies resulted in defensive carbine fire of such concentrated intensity that the attackers were compelled to fall back. Said Gall: *"They fought strong; they fought in line along the ridges."*

To the northwest the *Light Horse Troop* not only withstood the assaults by Two Moon, but also helped force Lame White Man's Cheyenne to remain in Greasy Grass Coulee. That enabled the rest of *L Troop* to rejoin its brother platoon on the South Knoll.

A quarter-mile to the east, the same kind of scenario unfolded with Wolf Tooth's group. Since being pushed off the Upland Ridge, it had been unable to gain ground against *F Troop*. Mounted but moving at a walk, the soldiers kept up a steady fire, leaving behind a trail of spent cartridges. Gall observed the movements

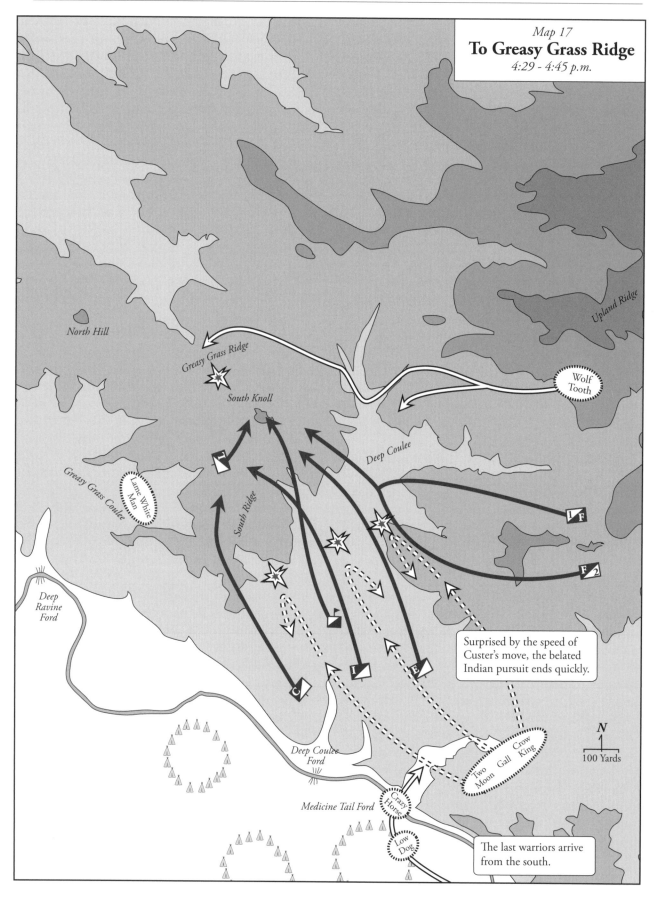

Map 17
To Greasy Grass Ridge
4:29 - 4:45 p.m.

Upland Ridge

North Hill

Greasy Grass Ridge

South Knoll

Wolf Tooth

Deep Coulee

Greasy Grass Coulee

Lame White Man

South Ridge

Deep Ravine Ford

Surprised by the speed of Custer's move, the belated Indian pursuit ends quickly.

N

100 Yards

Deep Coulee Ford

Two Moon Gall Crow King

Crazy Horse

Medicine Tail Ford

Low Dog

The last warriors arrive from the south.

of *2ND PLATOON* on the south face of the ridge and later indicated there was *"a now rapid, now slow march, according to the ground."*

As soon as the *F TROOP* platoons reunited at the Juncture – the confluence of the ravines between Upland and Greasy Grass Ridges – they dismounted. White Shield remembered, *"The troops remained there for only a few minutes. Crowded back, they crossed a deep gulch [Deep Coulee] and climbed the hill on the other side."*

The Wolf Tooth group was by then just a distant, if still menacing, presence on the opposite ridgeline. Then the Blackfoot faction broke away, taking a position overlooking the Juncture. Wolf Tooth and the rest of his braves continued toward the crest of the Greasy Grass, arriving there about seven minutes after the headquarters detachment had occupied the Knoll. On their approach the cavalrymen opened a heavy fire, even though those hostiles were actually still beyond effective range. *"Finally,"* said Gall, *"all the soldiers halted there."*

In the meantime the Oglala under Crazy Horse and Low Dog finally disengaged from their fight with Reno, departing that area at 4:35. Leaving behind about 100 outriders to patrol and keep watch, the remainder formed a fifth and final wave of reinforcements for the fight against Custer. Low Dog's 280 Agency Oglala and Crazy Horse's 400 Non-Agency Oglala, Brule, and Arapahoe tipped the odds against Custer to 11-to-1. The newcomers crossed Medicine Tail Ford just in time to see their fellow tribesmen return from the second failed foray, while the cavalry was getting situated in its new location.

Many Indians later recalled how the cavalrymen were *"all mixed in together"* when they reached their objective. The cavalry's situation was acute: outnumbered, surrounded, and ill-deployed. As things stood at 4:45, James Calhoun's *L TROOP* and the headquarters detachment stood atop South Knoll, with *F TROOP* about 80 yards down the eastern slope; some 150 yards due south were *E, I,* and *C TROOPS*. The units formed a roughly convex line extending west to east for a quarter-mile. Curley, who had remained with the headquarters, was shortly joined by the wounded interpreter: *"Boyer thought the order would [soon] be given to charge straight ahead, [to try to] drive the Indians form the ravine and try to find more favorable ground."*

Custer, though, had something else in mind. The men barely had time to catch their breath when they were again set in motion in a series of moves intended to further redress the line, disconcert the hostiles and, most importantly, reestablish contact with the rest of the regiment. The Indians below immediately noticed the new burst of activity. The troops had been afoot, but now climbed back into their saddles and divided into several groups. Said one warrior: *"The different groups of soldiers moved about a little on higher ground, some going toward the river and some away from it."*

At 4:46, Custer unleashed his new plan. Three troops simultaneously bound ahead, each in a different direction. Smith's *E TROOP* went past the summit to end in a position to cover the northwest approaches to the hill, while its vacated spot was occupied a minute later by Yates' *F TROOP*. Fanning out as they pushed west, Tom Custer's *C TROOP* split into two platoons, sweeping across the entire south rim of the Greasy Grass. That stunned Lame White Man's Agency Cheyenne, who were forced out of the coulee below and had to retire hastily toward Deep Ravine. Equally surprising was the sudden retreat of both platoons back to the Knoll after only a few minutes. Left behind, however, was a 12-man detail on West Ridge, apparently intended to keep the surrounding area under constant observation.

Simultaneously, Keogh's *I TROOP* plunged down into Deep Coulee, straight toward the massed formation under Gall a half-mile away. What seemed at first to be a mad rush quickly corrected itself as the cavalrymen deftly angled left toward the Blackfoot group, who were then situated above the Juncture. There Deep Coulee branches, a third of a mile from South Knoll. The Indians there rapidly moved out of harms way, while the soldiers rode up the coulee's north branch, then swung in an expansive arc across the entire eastern face of the Knoll. That move flanked Wolf Tooth, necessitating his abandonment of the crest of Greasy Grass Ridge for the safety of North Hill, even as the troopers reined up to the right of the *GRAY HORSE TROOP* at 4:55.

Gall noted the display of cavalry dexterity with both awe and puzzlement, only belatedly discerning through the dust that a detail of 14 men had separated from *I Troop*. Those soldiers made their way to the top of Upland Ridge in a circuitous attempt to break through to Benteen. The war chief would have instructed a party of his own to give chase, but the bypassed Blackfoot quickly had split into two bands, one closely following the bluecoats, the other attempting to cut them off from the south.

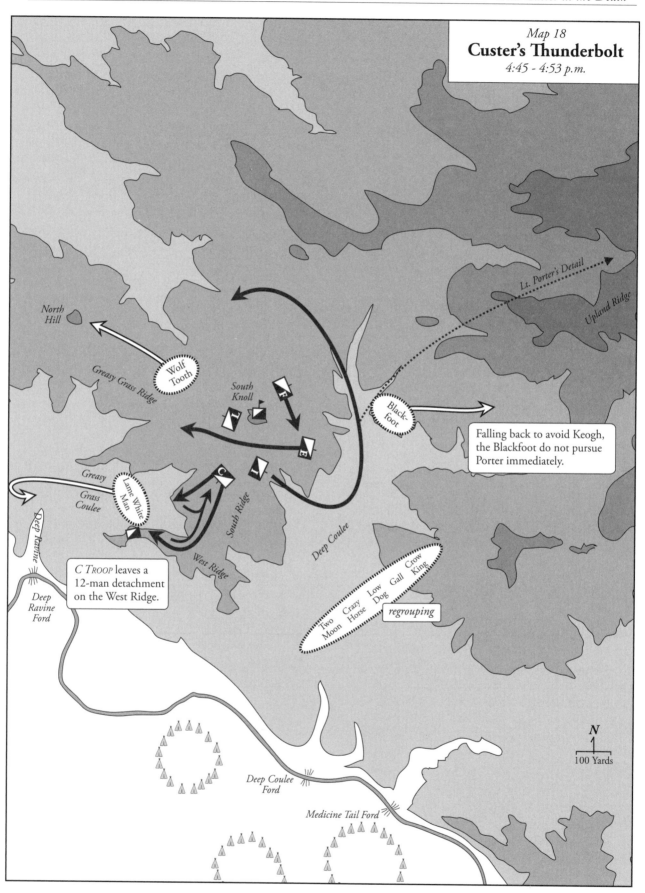

Map 18
Custer's Thunderbolt
4:45 - 4:53 p.m.

Lt. Porter's Detail

Upland Ridge

North
Hill

Greasy Grass Ridge

Wolf
Tooth

South
Knoll

F

I

E

C

I

Black-
foot

Falling back to avoid Keogh,
the Blackfoot do not pursue
Porter immediately.

Greasy
Grass
Coulee

Lame White
Man

South Ridge

Deep Coulee

Deep
Ravine

Deep
Ravine
Ford

C Troop leaves a
12-man detachment
on the West Ridge.

West Ridge

Two   Crazy   Low   Gall   Crow
Moon   Horse   Dog   King

regrouping

N

100 Yards

Deep Coulee
Ford

Medicine Tail Ford

Somewhere along the way eight of the troopers turned back and rejoined the battalion. The remaining six, probably led by Lt. James E. Porter, continued on their journey. Unfortunately, the swift ponies of one Blackfoot group blocked any access to the bluffs to the southeast, while the other group barred the way back to Custer. The bluecoats were fated to keep riding, unable to shake off their pursuers. Four of them, an officer and three enlisted, made their own "last stand" just six miles from where they started, while the remaining two continued east, the last of them falling at the end of a 15-mile chase. The soldiers, reported Gall, *"dashed toward the Wolf Mountains, but the young warriors got on their trail and they all were killed."*

With the exception of *I Troop's* last minute arrival at the north end of South Knoll, Custer's realigned defense was firmly established by the time the Indians launched their first organized and all-out attack at 4:54. Said Wooden Leg afterward: *"The troops extended themselves along the ridge."*

Held by *Troops I, E, C,* and *F,* the defense line ran for nearly 1,600 yards southward along much of the Greasy Grass ridge-line. The headquarters detachment and *L Troop* remained on the Knoll itself as combat reserve. Directly behind the line, to the northeast — which was clear of hostiles — were gathered the horse-holders and mounts. An Indian female named Pretty White Buffalo stated: *"The attackers who were left, still in large numbers, moved back from the river and waited"* for the next attack.

By now virtually all of the tribal bands — collectively some 2,400 braves — were gathered at distances averaging roughly a half-mile from Custer's strong-point. The Wolf Tooth group, a mixed bag of Sioux and Cheyenne, were on North Hill, while the Agency Cheyenne of Lame White Man dominated the lower slopes of Greasy Grass Ridge.

The greatest concentration was in the south. There a solid wall of Indians extended across a 1,000 yard front. Nearest to the river was Two Moon with the Non-Agency Cheyenne, Arapahoe and Gros Ventres. To their right stood Crazy Horse and the Non-Agency Oglala, the Brule, and Assiniboin. Next to them was Low Dog and the Agency Oglala, then Gall, leading half the Hunkpapa plus all the Blackfoot and Sans Arc. Finally, on the slopes of Upland Ridge, was Crow King with the remaining Hunkpapa, Santee, Yankton, Minniconju, and Two Kettle. Said Crow King: *"The Indian chiefs would give the 'Hi-Yi-Yi' [war cry] in a high pitch*

every time they charged. When this cry is given it is a command to all the warriors to watch the chief and follow his instructions. Then each chief rushed his horse against the white soldiers, and all the warriors did the same."

When the signal was given at 4:54, the tribesmen had a considerable distance to cross, so the possibility of surprise was lost. At first Custer's men simply stood and waited as the wave of Indians came toward them. When they got within range, the soldiers unleashed a torrent of lead that shattered the charge like a breakwater. The attackers then no longer came all at once, but in a series of successive rushes. *"We had them surrounded,"* said Two Moon, *"and first the Sioux and then the Cheyenne would charge them. In our first big charge we had all swept in together."*

Gall and other Indians stated later there were five such battering ram charges from the south; and quite possibly an equal number from the opposite side of the hill, each of which were met by numbers of defensive volleys. One of the attackers noted that only after they actually had reached the slopes of the Greasy Grass *"did the troops become provoked enough to fire, and the warriors were then forced to beat a hasty retreat."*

Crow King
Sub-chief of the Hunkpapa

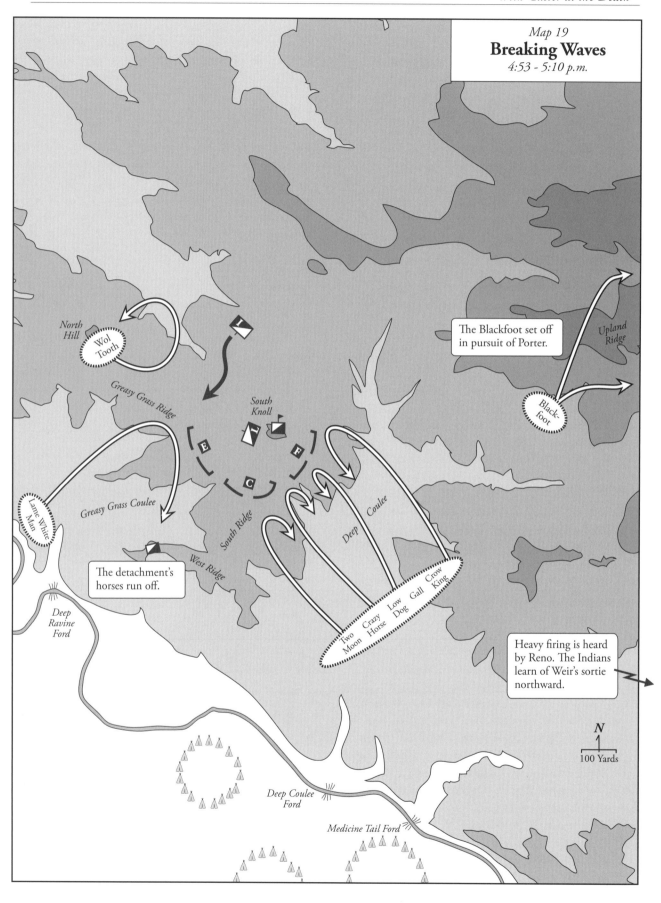

Map 19
Breaking Waves
4:53 - 5:10 p.m.

North Hill

Wol Tooth

The Blackfoot set off in pursuit of Porter.

Upland Ridge

Black-foot

Greasy Grass Ridge

South Knoll

E   I   F

C

Greasy Grass Coulee

Lame White Man

South Ridge

Deep Coulee

West Ridge

The detachment's horses run off.

Two   Crazy   Low   Gall   Crow
Moon   Horse   Dog   King

Deep Ravine Ford

Heavy firing is heard by Reno. The Indians learn of Weir's sortie northward.

N

100 Yards

Deep Coulee Ford

Medicine Tail Ford

Gall
War Chief of the Hunkpapa

Captain Myles W. Keogh
Commanding I Troop, 7th Cavalry

In spite of the stout defense, the Indians repeatedly rallied and returned to the attack. The sounds of the fight were easily audible to those on the distant Heights, which prompted one of Reno's officers, Capt. Thomas Weir, to set out with his own troop *(D)* on a journey toward the High Bluffs. It was a move seen and quickly reported by the outriders left behind to patrol the valley.

Gall and the others made one attack after another, only to be forced back each time. Through it all there were displays of raw, brazen courage. Leaders like Yellow Nose, Crazy Horse, and Comes In Sight got close to the soldiers but failed in their attempts to penetrate the line. The soldiers were equally undaunted. Among the most conspicuous was a mounted officer, possibly Lt. John Crittenden of *L Troop*, who rode back and forth behind the line shouting orders and encourage-

ment to his men. Though one horse went down, he quickly sprang to another, only to be fatally wounded shortly thereafter.

Above all, it was *I Troop's* dramatic and last-minute arrival at the north end of Custer's line that saved the position from being enveloped by the converging forces of Wolf Tooth and Lame White Man. Getting in place just as the attackers were about to engage them, Keogh's men dismounted, held their horses by the bridles and pelted the enemy with bullets, just barely repulsing them.

By about 5:10, it finally became apparent the attackers were getting nowhere. Crazy Horse, his pony completely played out, heard word of other cavalry approaching along the bluff tops (Weir would reach the Peak in a matter of minutes). The Indians made the decision to disengage and reconsider their options.

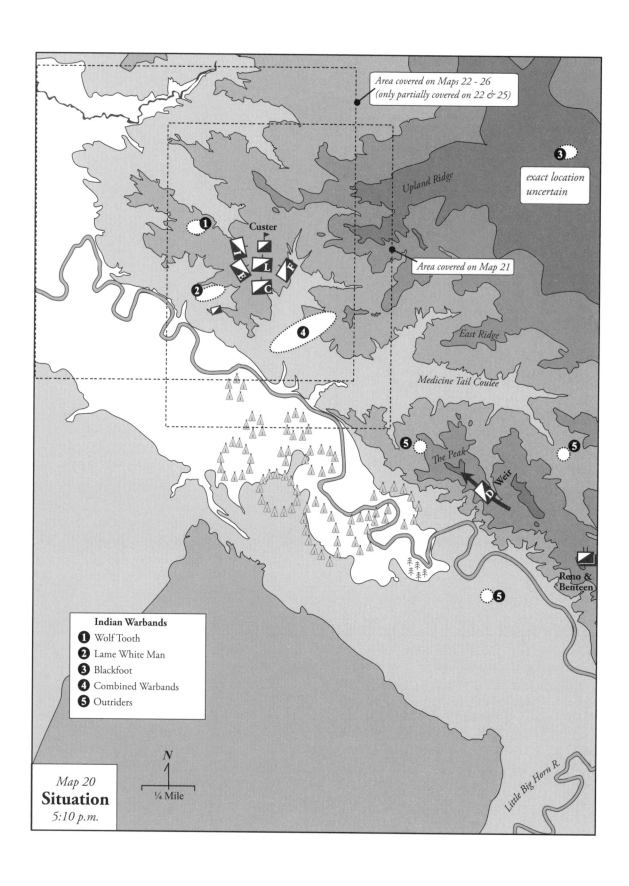

Area covered on Maps 22 - 26
(only partially covered on 22 & 25)

exact location
uncertain

Upland Ridge

Custer

Area covered on Map 21

East Ridge

Medicine Tail Coulee

The Peak

D Weir

Reno &
Benteen

Indian Warbands

1 Wolf Tooth
2 Lame White Man
3 Blackfoot
4 Combined Warbands
5 Outriders

N

¼ Mile

Little Big Horn R.

Map 20
Situation
5:10 p.m.

Chapter Four
Lower Valley Foray
5:10 p.m. - 6:25 p.m.

Map 21
Interlude
5:10 - 5:20 p.m.

North Hill

Wolf Tooth

Greasy Grass Ridge

I

South Knoll

E   L   F

C

Greasy Grass Coulee

Lame White Man

West Ridge

South Ridge

Deep Coulee

Two Moon Crazy Horse Low Dog Gall Crow King

Deep Ravine Ford

The *C Troop* detachment is flushed out and run down. The last two men are killed at the river's edge.

Deep Coulee Ford

Medicine Tail Ford

Upland Ri

N
100 Yards

Shortly after the Indian attacks were suspended, Gall called a war council. There was agreement among the chiefs that the cavalry activity on the bluffs (Weir) was of secondary importance to the threat posed by the enemy occupying South Knoll. They suspected Custer might strike the village via Deep Ravine. At that moment the greater proportion of the assembled warriors, perhaps 80 percent, were to the south of Greasy Grass Ridge. Everyone realized a new deployment was needed, which resulted in a new division of command. Henceforth Crow King, Gall, Crazy Horse, and Lame White Man would share those responsibilities.

Not far away, Custer also was reconsidering his position. He realized quick action was needed to retrieve the initiative before it was too late. He could not depend on the rest of the regiment for assistance. (There was no indication he was aware of Capt. Weir's presence on the Peak, but he may have inferred from the pause in the action that Lt. Porter's detachment had gotten through to Benteen). The pause in the action gave him a chance, though, and he was never one to willingly pass up a fleeting battlefield opportunity. He held a hasty officers' conference at 5:15.

Curley stood nearby, watching as Mitch Boyer joined the assemblage: *"I saw Mitch talking with the general."* Custer announced his intention to try another crossing farther downstream. Boyer tried but failed to dissuade Custer from the undertaking. As the meeting broke up, Tom Custer, also understanding the risks, restated his brother's earlier suggestion that Boyer and Curley had done their jobs and could leave. Boyer then walked over to the Crow scout, pointed to the battalion commander and said in angry frustration: *"That man will stop at nothing. He's going to take us right down into the village where the Sioux have many more warriors than we do. We have no chance at all."*

Nor, for that matter, did Boyer expect the rest of the regiment to come up and relieve them, as the general seemed to be hoping. Nevertheless, Boyer told Curley he was going along with Custer, despite his own misgivings, and said: *"Curley, you are young and don't know much about fighting. I advise you to leave us."*

Gesturing toward the hills to the east as he spoke, he finished: *"Ride back over the trail a-ways, then go to one of the high points yonder. Watch a while and see if the Sioux are beating us."* Curley urged Boyer to come with

Mitch Boyer
Scout attached to 7TH CAVALRY

Curley
Scout attached to 7TH CAVALRY

him, but the latter declined, saying he was too badly wounded for such an effort. He would stay and fight it out.

While their leaders talked, most of the fighting men on both sides took what advantage they could from the lull. For a few, the action continued in deadly earnest.

The mounted portion of Lame White Man's Agency Cheyenne moved against the isolated 12-man *C Troop* detail, whose horses evidently had run off. Those men began pushing along West Ridge in an attempt to rejoin their comrades, only to be caught in mid-move. Two Eagles stated the ridge-line became the site *"of a great running fight,"* and that a group of 10-to-12 men worked their way south, while Custer and the rest —

too far away and with too little time to react — could only watch as the tragedy within a tragedy unfolded. Curley would never forget the sight. The hostiles circled around and cut off those men, *"a dozen or more soldiers…in a ravine fighting with Sioux [and Cheyenne] all around them."*

The small group was outnumbered at least five or six to one, and they were forced to make their way down a small cut on the far side of West Ridge. There most of them were over-powered and slain. Somehow two managed to get as far as the river, where they also lost their lives.

The conclave of chiefs broke up at 5:25, and the Indian redeployment got underway moments later. Crow King, together with half the Hunkpapa, Santee,

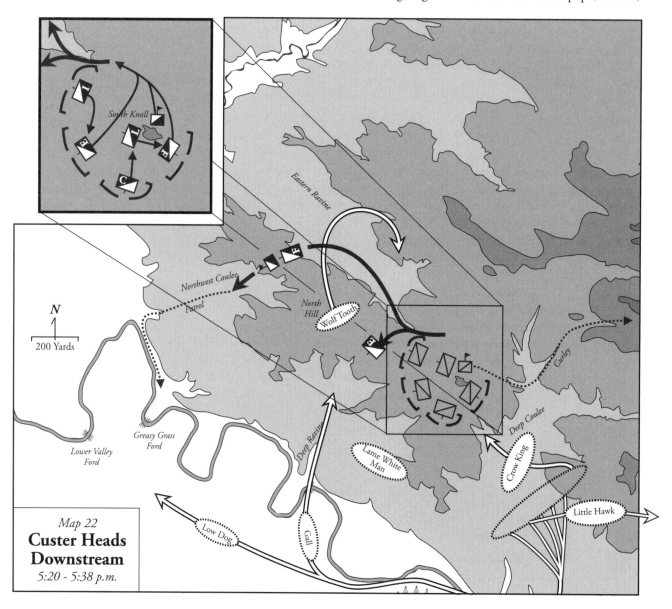

Map 22
Custer Heads Downstream
5:20 - 5:38 p.m.

and Yankton, advanced to the base of South Knoll and dismounted. They stayed behind to discourage any renewed bluecoat drive toward Medicine Tail Ford. At the same time about half the Brule, led by Little Hawk, separated from their brethren, moving to the western tip of East Ridge. There, due north of the Peak and overlooking Medicine Tail Coulee, they would keep the High Bluffs under surveillance.

The bulk of the Indians rode toward the Medicine Tail Ford. First across was Crazy Horse with the Non-Agency Oglala, the Assiniboin, and the remaining Brule under Iron Star. Right behind followed his close ally Two Moon with the Non-Agency Cheyenne, Arapahoe, and Gros Ventres. Gall, heading a force of Hunkpapa, Blackfoot, Sans Arc, Minniconju, and Two Kettle, came next, with Low Dog's Agency Oglala last.

Crazy Horse and Two Moon verged left, returning to their village camp circles, Low Dog moved west, but stayed on the 'Indian' side of the river to continue to cooperate with Crazy Horse, as he had done during the fight against Reno. Keeping with the plan, the Agency Oglala took station within the wide open wickiup section of the lower village, while Gall once again crossed over to the east side of the river, this time via Deep Ravine, and there combined his force with that of Lame White Man. By 5:38 all of the war parties had arrived at their new areas. The realignment placed half the Indians on the slopes of Greasy Grass Ridge, another third on the west bank, and the rest to the southeast.

While the Indians were on the move, the Custer battalion was engaged in a seemingly chaotic ballet. Yates' *F Troop* pulled off the line, to be replaced by *L Troop*. Yates, along with Custer and the headquarters detachment, formed Custer's main maneuvering force. The column went 150 yards down the northeast slope of the Knoll to a jump-off point. They were followed by Smith's *E Troop*, whose place in line was taken by *I Troop* sidling left. C Troop pulled back slight so that three troops – I, C, L, commanded in Custer's absence by Myles Keogh of *I Troop* – formed a tight perimeter around the peak of the knoll. Their horses were on the opposite slope, in comparative safety.

At about 5:25, Keogh's men unleashed a prolonged burst of small arms fire, which was intended to distract the hostiles and cloak Custer's movements. With that the general's command got underway. As they moved out, Boyer handed Curley a pair of field glasses and shook hands. Then he mounted a newly-acquired horse and rode off to rejoin the general, waving his hat in farewell. Curley watched the headquarters and *F Troop* move off, turning down into Eastern Ravine, then noticed *E Troop*, dismounted, heading left to occupy the crest of Greasy Grass Ridge.

The firing from Keogh's line and the movement of *E Troop* had had their intended effect. The war chiefs particularly were alarmed by *E Troop's* seizure of the ridge top, fearing the bluecoats were about to launch the anticipated drive down Deep Ravine before it could be blocked. The Wolf Tooth group, however, suspected they were actually the next target of the whites and hastily fled north to Eastern Ridge.

Ignoring them, Custer skirted past North Hill, then moved over Far Ridge, finally coming to a halt again in Northwest Coulee, about half a mile from the river. It was an ideal spot, effectively concealing the first section from Gall's scrutiny. In fact, at the time of their arrival, the nearest group of hostiles had begun crossing Medicine Tail Ford just three minutes before.

The general's tactical sleight of hand had given him the freedom of action he had sought, but he was hampered by the fact he had no idea as to where a usable crossing point might be. The deceptively gentle sloping terrain ahead of him, as with much of the battlefield, terminated in a sheer, vertical drop, and the Little Bighorn itself also had a tendency to hug the base of the escarpment. To clarify the situation, Custer dispatched a patrol from *F Troop* at 5:32 to explore the riverbank.

Curley had set off in the opposite shortly after Custer moved. He followed the same path taken earlier by the ill-fated detachment of Lt. Porter. The young Crow, entirely on his own, found what was actually the only way out: due east to the top of Upland Ridge, approximately one and a quarter miles from South Knoll. *"When I went out there were no Sioux in front....I took [a path] up the coulee to the head of the distant ridge."*

While en route he came across the corpse of a warrior who evidently had been killed during the earlier pursuit of Porter's unit. He confiscated the hostile's weapons and continued on his way, reaching the top of the ridge, where he stopped for a while to observe the fighting with his binoculars, just as Boyer had suggested. Though he could not make out much detail, he soon was forced to conclude the soldiers were being annihilated. Departing, he traveled to the Yellowstone River, where he happened on the crew of an army supply boat. There he told, as best he could, the first word of the disaster to the outside world, only to be met with disbelief.

Meanwhile, in the upper valley of the Little Big-horn, Capt. Benteen departed High Hill with three troops at 5:30. (A messenger bearing news of the move reached Crow King, Gall, and Crazy Horse around 6:00). Benteen's column reached the Peak at 5:45, to Weir's great relief; a *D Troop* patrol scouting to the northwest had just been chased back by Little Hawk's Brule.

The new arrivals were the spearhead for a potential link up with Custer, but Benteen was uncertain of his next move. From the Peak the distant battlefield was almost entirely obscured by a thick haze of dust and smoke, with little movement visible of any kind. By this time, activity around South Knoll had diminished to a veritable siege; the nexus of battle had moved farther north with Custer.

For a time after Custer's departure, the troopers on the Knoll had produced a steady, effective stream of bullets that kept the Indians from encroaching on the western slope of the Greasy Grass. At 5:43, suddenly, the right of the cavalry line, *E Troop,* vanished from the ridge crest. The troopers, now mounted, and making no attempt to conceal themselves, reappeared a moment later riding northwest along the face of North Hill toward the river. They rode, said Two Moon, *"beyond where the monument stands [today], down into the valley until we could not see them."*

Even more baffling to the Indians was another retrograde move by Keogh's right wing. These maneuvers together left the ridge crest wide open. Neither Gall nor Lame White Man made any immediate attempt to take advantage of the situation, but Wolf Tooth's group

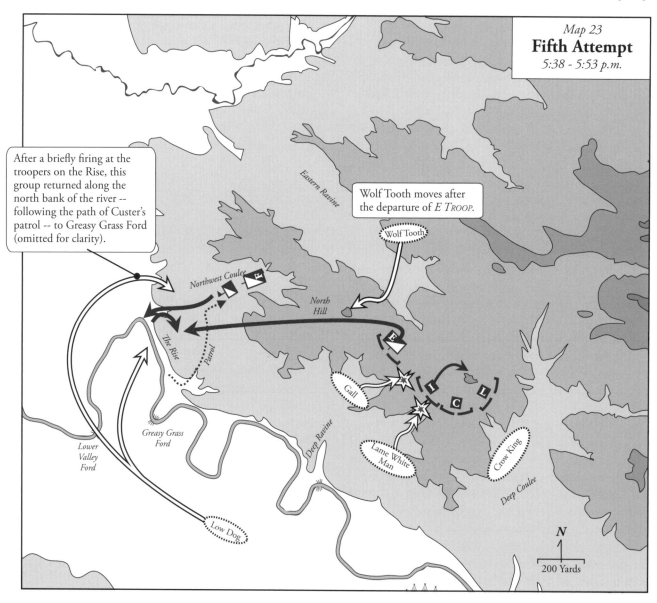

Map 23
Fifth Attempt
5:38 - 5:53 p.m.

After a briefly firing at the troopers on the Rise, this group returned along the north bank of the river -- following the path of Custer's patrol -- to Greasy Grass Ford (omitted for clarity).

Wolf Tooth moves after the departure of *E Troop.*

quickly reoccupied North Hill. Once there, the Indians discovered all the cavalry had moved well beyond the range of their weapons.

Southward down the slope from North Hill, Gall's mixed group of Hunkpapa, Blackfoot, Sans Arc, Minniconju, and Two Kettle were positioned to the left of Lame White Man's Agency Cheyenne. The Indians soon found that although half the available braves were gathered in front of Keogh's heavily outnumbered whites, the cavalry's firepower was sufficient to preclude going forward. Lame White Man had tried to do so, and the attempt was brutally rebuffed. As a result he was held to the lower reaches of the ridge, a circumstance in which Gall and his followers likewise soon found themselves. *"The warriors all dismounted and began to fight,"* said Wooden Leg, *"leaving their ponies in the gullies safe from the fight."*

In fact, not all the Indians dismounted; some remained on horseback to keep a better eye on the soldiers and to counter any thrust toward the encampment. The majority, though, chose to fight on foot. Leaving behind their ponies, they wasted little time in dashing forward and dropping to the ground. Taking whatever advantage they could from the undulating terrain, random sagebrush, and obscuring haze of powder-smoke and dust, they began long-range sniping at the soldiers above.

The troopers fought back in a like manner. One Sioux youth later remembered:

> *They held their ground bravely and fought desperately… They stood shoulder to shoulder in solid companies and their ranks were broken only by those who were shot [down]. On the other hand, the Indians were scattered over a range of land. Some were behind rocks and kept up a continuous fire into the solid companies. The companies neither made any charge nor attempted to fall back.*

After a time, the fighting slowed to a stalemate. There was nothing the Indians could do to alter the situation as long as the troopers held firm to so much of the ridgeline. The warriors hesitated to come to grips with the enemy, content for a time to wait and watch.

A thousand yards to the west, the *F Troop* river patrol had returned after a 13-minute ride, having found two prospective fording sites. With the *Gray Horse Troop's* arrival on his flank, Custer now had a powerful assault force collected, with no enemy in sight.

He headed his column for the nearest potential ford, where the river looped to the southwest onto an expansive flood plain. Ever mindful of what might happen if Gall suddenly swept in from behind, the two cavalry columns converged as the seconds passed.

F Troop reached the riverbank, while *E Troop* occupied a low rise just behind to give fire support. The fire support was needed, because far from being empty, the opposite bank swarmed with Indians. Off to the west, another party of mounted Indians took the cavalry under fire.

The Indians were Low Dog's Agency Oglala. After crossing the river during the Indian redeployment, Low Dog's warriors had remained in the lower village where, in the words of Pretty White Buffalo, they had *"moved back from the river and waited for the attack."* Far from biding their time, pickets were sent to watch every possible crossing point. Those guarding Greasy Grass Ford had seen the cavalry reconnaissance at about 5:40 and rushed back with the news.

Gathering more than 300 warriors, Low Dog raced west. On reaching the narrow bends in the river, the group split. One group moved to the right to take up

Low Dog
War Chief of the (Agency) Oglala

positions along the west bank (the group that greeted Custer's arrival at the river), while the other, led by the war chief himself, crossed the stream at Lower Valley Ford.

The latter group saw Custer's column coming onto Greasy Grass Rise, and brazenly moved to cut across their path. One Sioux later reported: *"Custer [was] fighting…and chased the Indians back toward the river."* From atop North Hill, nearly a mile away, it appeared to Wolf Tooth that *"some of the warriors had come across [the river] and began firing at the soldiers from the brush in the river bottom."*

Low Dog had in fact wheeled about, heading west, down a ravine toward the river, then east through the brush and cottonwood trees lining the banks. He did not stop to fight, but continued south toward Greasy

Grass Ford. It was the closest access to the opposite bank in the vicinity, and the only other location spotted by the earlier cavalry patrol.

As Custer approached the northernmost bend of the stream, the Indians hiding amid the undergrowth could see clearly that his troopers were apprehensive, but also that they were not faltering. Ohiyesa remembered Custer *"was spotted as he emerged into the open and headed for the river. The Indians shouted a warning: 'Wow! Wow! Here they come!'"*

The cavalry clearly could not cross in the face of such strong opposition, though the tribesmen right on the bank were driven back. Some troopers dismounted to examine the bank for another place to cross. It soon became clear the area was unsuitable, and all the soldiers got back in their saddles. All the while both sides

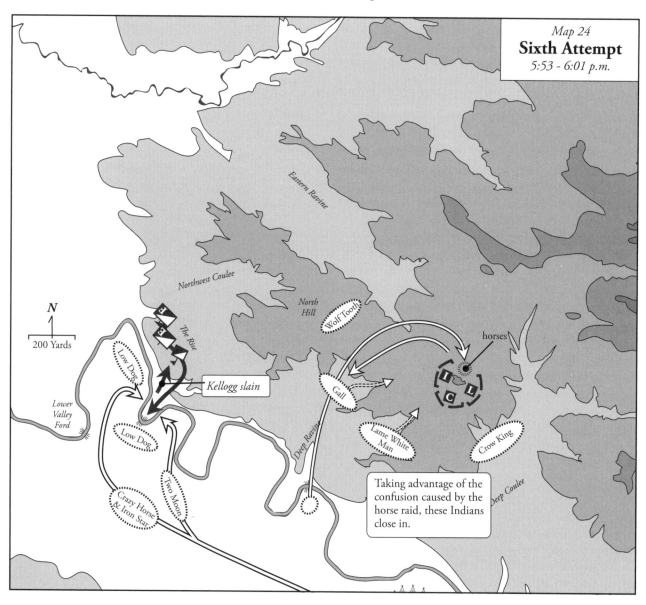

Map 24
Sixth Attempt
5:53 - 6:01 p.m.

Eastern Ravine

Northwest Coulee

North Hill

Wolf Tooth

N

200 Yards

The Rise

Low Dog

Lower Valley Ford

Low Dog

Two Moon

Crazy Horse & Iron Star

Kellogg slain

Deep Ravine

Gall

Lame White Man

horses

I C L

Crow King

Deep Coulee

Taking advantage of the confusion caused by the horse raid, these Indians close in.

kept up a steady fire, until Custer reluctantly terminated the attack at 5:52 and pulled back to the rise,

Five miles away, Reno was just leaving the Heights with a troop of cavalry. Even as all that was taking place, Crazy Horse received word of Benteen's arrival on the Peak and Custer's attack to the north. After considering the risks, he and Two Moon led their warriors toward Long Hair.

Pausing only briefly on the rise, Custer quickly launched another attack – his sixth attempted crossing of the day – toward the second ford observed by the patrol. Leaving *F Troop* behind to prevent any more interference from the west, the headquarters detachment and the *Gray Horse Troop* spurred forward, riding four abreast. They moved down a ravine, then west along a peninsula-like bend in the river that was 80 yards wide and 250 yards long. It was a potential death trap, fringed by a thick barrier of trees and undergrowth, but the troopers reached their objective unhindered.

Custer saw immediately Greasy Grass Ford was everything he could have hoped for, and readily moved out across the Little Big Horn with Mitch Boyer riding to his one side and the guidon bearer and bugler on the other.

Just then Low Dog's braves opened fire. Boyer, wearing a distinctive spotted calf vest, was hit immediately. The general began firing his Remington sporting rifle, and the troopers also began shooting in the direction of the concealed enemy to their front. No sooner had that new fighting begun than the firing reached an intensity that forced the bluecoats to stop in midstream, just as trumpeter Henry Dose went down. Several soldiers jumped into the water to save him and Boyer, dragging them back to dry land. Both men were still alive but badly wounded.

The situation was about to get worse. Crazy Horse and Two Moon had arrived and were riding along the banks on either side of the peninsula. Unable to make headway at the crossing, and on the verge of being caught in a deadly crossfire between hundreds of Indians, Custer saw how hopeless things had become. He ordered his men, still mounted and blazing away, to retreat, leaving the dying Boyer and Dose behind. It was 6:00 p.m.

As the troopers fled they ran a bristling gauntlet of fire. The Indians, said Wolf Tooth, *"began firing from the brush in the river bottom. That made the soldiers turn northward, back to the high ground."* During the re-

treat, journalist Mark Kellogg became a casualty in the fighting he had come along to write about, cut down a quarter mile from the ford.

Custer soon reached Greasy Grass Rise, and there deployed to meet an onrushing flood of Non-Agency Cheyenne under Two Moon, who had followed in hot pursuit. The Indians' triumphant rush was short-lived, however, as a torrent of small arms fire forced them to take cover wherever they could. The standoff would continue for the next quarter-hour.

Four miles to the south, Capt. McDougall had departed from the Heights with the last elements of the regiment: two cavalry troops, some wounded soldiers, and the pack train.

While Custer's action was winding down, Keogh's was heating up. The departure of *E Troop* and the subsequent contraction of the line into a horseshoe-shaped perimeter gave Gall an unexpected opportunity, and like Custer, he would not let it pass. Gall and Lame White Man pushed their braves forward to seize the central area of the Greasy Grass Ridge. *"Some of the warriors dismounted near the crest of the hill,"* said Gall. *"Mounted warriors were lower down the hillside."*

Linking up with Crow King on the right and Wolf Tooth on the left, the Indians for the first time set up a continuous battlefront. This enabled a readjustment of Indian tactics. Lame White Man suggested that instead of a prolonged firefight, they should begin to lay down a crossfire on the soldiers while extending their lines gradually to complete the encirclement. When the time was right they would all rise up and take the hill by storm.

Gall at first liked the idea, but then noticed a weak spot in Keogh's perimeter: its exposed, but still unassailed, northern face. There every fourth trooper held tightly to the reins of the horses, while the rest of the soldiers were on the firing line. Gall rode back downhill, gathering horsemen to him as he went. *"When he recrossed the river,"* recalled Pretty White Buffalo, *"many warriors followed his party, and we heard him tell his men to frighten the horses of the soldiers, which were held in small bunches."*

Reversing direction, Gall led the warriors up and over the summit into Eastern Ravine. *"We tried to kill the horse-holders,"* he said, *"and then, by waving blankets and shouting, we scared the horses."*

The result was pandemonium as the panicky mounts became increasingly troublesome. *"Some horses, shot or pierced by arrows, plunged around,"* said Wooden

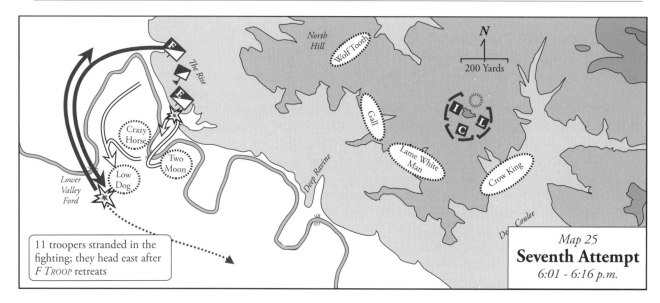

11 troopers stranded in the fighting; they head east after *F TROOP* retreats

Map 25
Seventh Attempt
6:01 - 6:16 p.m.

Leg, and many broke free, tearing through the skirmish line and down toward the river, where they were captured by Indian women and other noncombatants.

But Gall's triumph did not last, as the cavalrymen brought their carbines to bear. Said Two Kettle war chief Runs The Enemy: *"The return fire was so strong the Sioux had to retreat back over the hill [ridge] again."*

Though the raid had been a severe blow to Keogh, – a third of the horses lost, and with them the precious saddlebag stores of ammunition – none of his 90 men, as far as can be determined, were killed or even severely wounded in it. The Indian probe only caused them to adopt less exposed stances. Henceforth, rather than standing, they sat, knelt, lay prone, or concealed themselves behind a barricade of horse carcasses atop the Knoll. That change actually worked to their advantage, since the Indians began to have a more difficult time seeing them. *"The Indians stayed away from the open ground as much as possible,"* observed Red Feather, *"using whatever cover was available — coulees, sagebrush, even clumps of wild grass."*

Under those circumstances the only way for the warriors to get off a rifle shot was to jump to their feet. In contrast, the soldiers needed only to watch and wait for targets. Even bows and arrows were of little use to the attackers, for though they might reach 200 yards with a high arc, their effective range was much more limited. All the Indians could do was keep up an inexorable, creeping advance. Kate Bighead, a noncombatant with the Cheyenne tribe, later commented: *"There was a long time — the old men say it must have been an hour and a half of fighting — [just] shooting — with not much happening on either side."*

While *E TROOP* and Two Moon had traded repulses around Greasy Grass Ford, *F TROOP'S* front had remained quiet. The Indians thus were put under the false impression the unit had departed the first crossing point.

After *E TROOP'S* repulse, with no sign of any other bluecoats in the vicinity, Low Dog pulled back his two Agency Oglala groups, reuniting at 6:06. He failed to notice that *F TROOP* was indeed still in the area, and once again on the move, this time farther west.

Yates' troop moved along at a brisk pace, following the well-worn trail to the south toward what they hoped would be a river crossing. They were able to skirt past Low Dog's hostiles, who were gathering a quarter-mile off. Not until they came close to their objective — Lower Valley Ford — did the Sioux finally notice the movement and rush to intercept them. *F TROOP* continued to gallop without pause, actually crossing the stream at 6:11, only to be hit from the left by Low Dog's counter-stroke.

After a short and furious melee, Yates was forced to retrace his route. In the chaos, 11 of his men were separated from the rest. Left with no alternative, the stranded troopers attempted to continue to the south, the only avenue seemingly still open to them. Said Gall: *"They…were chased upstream…toward the village…."*

Atop the Rise, Custer watched Yates retreat along the river. Realizing his offensive had failed, he ordered the troops on the Rise to withdraw as well. Two Moon's band, said Ohiyesa, *"at once opened up on the soldiers, who were gradually retreating toward the Ridge, one half mile from the river bank."*

Reuniting at 6:19, Custer's strike force retired in more or less the same direction from which it had come a half-hour earlier. However, instead of following the Northwest Coulee, they veered right, coming to a halt on Low Ridge, just below North Hill.

With the immediate threat posed by Long Hair defused, Crazy Horse too planned to retrace his steps. He had to keep Custer from rejoining Keogh, and to discourage Reno from coming to Custer's rescue.

With those objectives in mind, he instructed Two Moon – already following Custer's retreat – to keep up the pressure on Low Ridge. The rest of the Indians who had repulsed Custer would recross the river to get back into the main fight. At 6:18. Crazy Horse moved south. He was followed moments later by Low Dog, now accompanied by Iron Star's Brule.

After crossing the river, Crazy Horse led his warriors across Greasy Grass Ridge, passing between the dismounted braves under Gall and Wolf Tooth. Circling around the latter, the force split, coming to a halt on either side of North Hill.

Down the slope, Custer faced a foreboding sight. Crazy Horse's unhindered sweep over the Greasy Grass

placed a large Indian force to his front, while Two Moon's men were crowding in from behind. Between the commands of Custer and Keogh, the entire western slope of the ridge was occupied by Gall and Lame White Man. *"Up to this time,"* said Ohiyesa, *"Custer did not seem to comprehend the danger before him. But when one company of his command reached the summit of the Ridge, it quickly found that the brow of the hill was held by Indians."*

Once again, the general's troopers dismounted and formed a defensive semi-circle: E Troop in the northwest; F Troop in the south; the headquarters detachment and riderless horses in the center. *"The soldiers,"* remembered Wolf Tooth, *"went back in the direction they had come from, and stopped when they got to where the cemetery is now. And they waited there 20 minutes or more."*

This phase of the battle came to an end with two dramatic events, one small and one large. The former occurred first, in the Deep Ravine. As Crazy Horse had passed through the ravine, he and his men had failed to notice the 11 men of *F Troop*, still trying to re-

First Lieutenant Algernon E. Smith
Commanding E Troop, 7th Cavalry

Captain George W. Yates
Commanding F Troop, 7th Cavalry

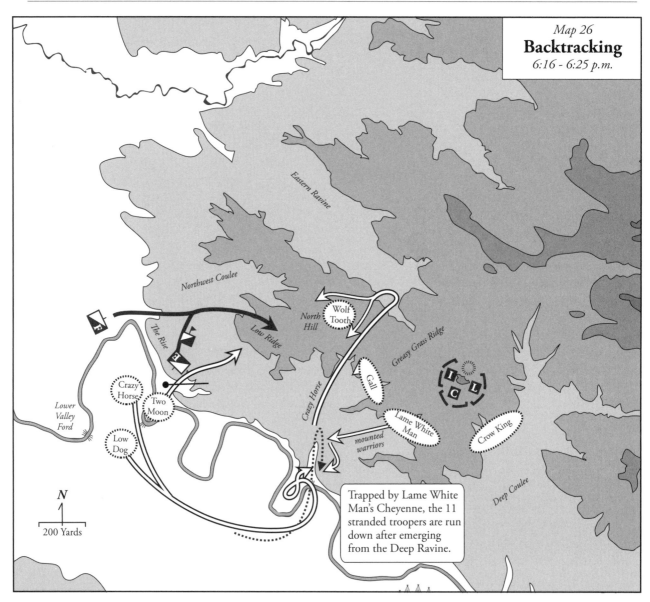

Map 26
Backtracking
6:16 - 6:25 p.m.

Trapped by Lame White Man's Cheyenne, the 11 stranded troopers are run down after emerging from the Deep Ravine.

turn to their unit. After the Non-Agency Oglala swept past them, the troopers emerged from Deep Ravine to find their path blocked by Gall's contingent. Turning right, toward South Knoll, they found the route barred by the Cheyenne of Lame White Man, who spotted the soldiers and gave chase. Quickly backtracking, the small group soon came to a final, fearsome discovery: the combined force of Low Dog and Iron Star was rushing across the river directly in front of them.

Equally astonished by the unexpected appearance of the bluecoats, the war chief surmised they might be the tip of the anticipated thrust down Deep Ravine. *"They came at us like a thunderbolt. I never saw men so brave nor fearless as those white warriors,"* he later said.

Caught completely off guard by the brazen rush of the cavalrymen, he and his followers were equally non-

plussed to find they were the spearhead of a phantom attack. With the Oglala to their front and the Cheyenne rapidly closing from behind, the troopers dismounted at a point 150 yards from the river. Low Dog recalled:

We retreated until we got all our men together [again]. [Then] every man whipped another man's horse, and we rode right up to them. As we rushed them, the white warriors dismounted to fire, but they did very poor shooting. They had their horses on one arm…but the horses were so frightened that they pulled the men around and a great many of the[ir] shots went up in the air and did us no harm. The white warriors stood their ground bravely, and none of them made any attempt to get away.

The fight ended less than a minute after it had begun, with all 11 troopers cut down. Instead of continuing north, Low Dog and Iron Star turned south, toward the High Bluffs, where the remainder of the *7TH CAVALRY* apparently was on the move. Should they arrive, the Indians' hard-won advantage against Custer would go for nought.

Just minutes earlier, Reno had reached the Peak, followed shortly thereafter by McDougall. With half the regiment concentrated and ready for action, Reno convened an officers' conference to decide what ought to be done next: ride forward, remain in place, or withdraw.

With so much dust hanging over the battlefield it was difficult to discern Custer's true situation. The only hostiles who could be seen were those in Crow King's party, hugging the eastern slope of South Knoll. The only shooting that could be heard, though, seemed to be coming from a great distance off, and even that had ceased by 6:15. What they heard of course, was the rattles of gunfire from the various ill-fated downstream crossing attempts.

Shortly thereafter, they began to notice disturbing activity to the northwest. As one of them recalled: *"Clouds of dust rose from all parts of the field and the[n] horsemen converged toward our position."*

What they were seeing was the return trip of Custer and the Indians, culminating with Crazy Horse surmounting Greasy Grass Ridge. Another stream of Indians (Low Dog and Iron Star) seemed to be heading in their direction. Deducing that Custer had been driven off, and convinced that a mass of hostiles was heading his way, Reno gave the order to pull back at 6:21. Though hastily improvised, the retreat went quickly. The last of his troopers would be off the Peak by 6:33. Low Dog and the Brule, reunited under Little Hawk, pursued and harassed the cavalry all the way back to High Hill, where they would remain for the rest of the battle. Custer's battalion was left to its own devices.

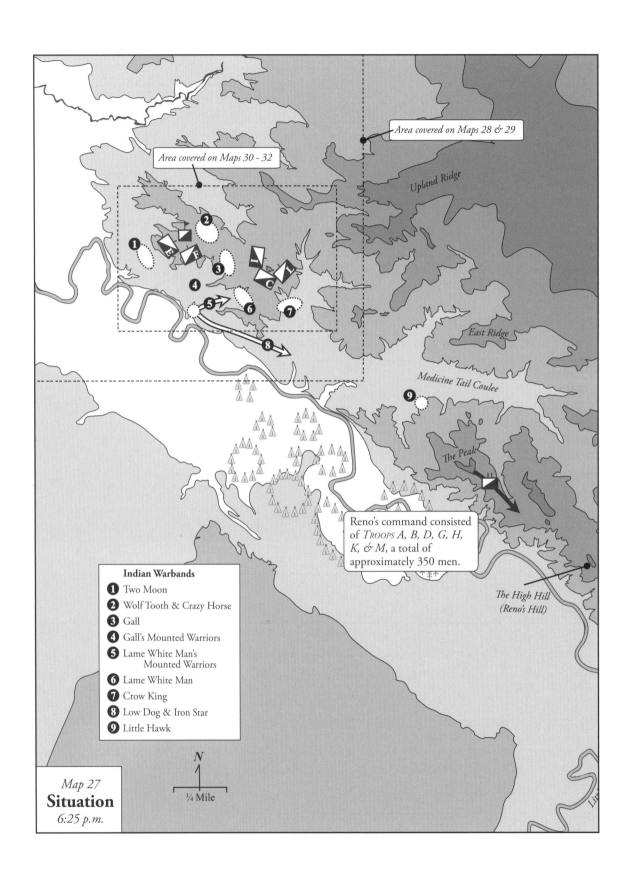

Area covered on Maps 28 & 29

Area covered on Maps 30 - 32

Upland Ridge

East Ridge

Medicine Tail Coulee

The Peak

Reno's command consisted of *Troops A, B, D, G, H, K, & M*, a total of approximately 350 men.

The High Hill (Reno's Hill)

Indian Warbands

1 Two Moon
2 Wolf Tooth & Crazy Horse
3 Gall
4 Gall's Mounted Warriors
5 Lame White Man's Mounted Warriors
6 Lame White Man
7 Crow King
8 Low Dog & Iron Star
9 Little Hawk

N

¼ Mile

Map 27
Situation
6:25 p.m.

Chapter Five

Back to the Greasy Grass
6:25 p.m. - 7:42 p.m.

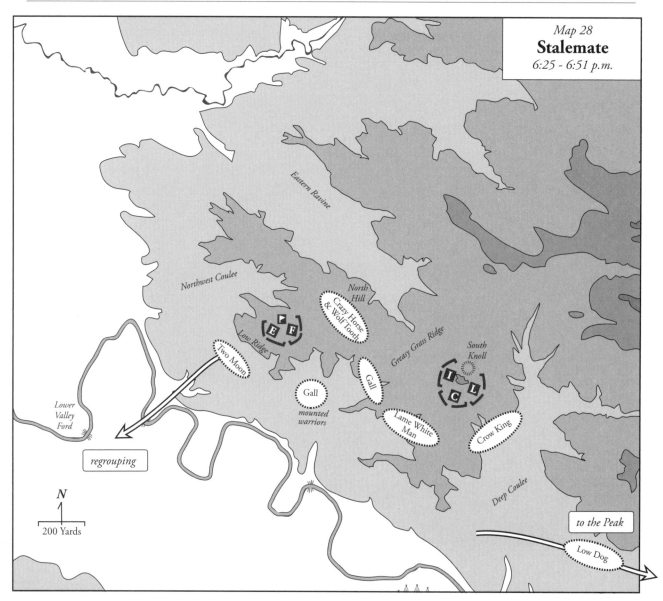

Map 28
Stalemate
6:25 - 6:51 p.m.

By this time, Custer's battalion was down to 173 men, 82 on North Hill with Custer, the remaining 91 with Keogh on South Knoll. Each group formed a perimeter, facing threats everywhere, but focused toward the ridge between the cavalry positions.

This mass of Indians – nearly 1,800 of the 2,600 warriors actively engaged in the battle – formed three main groups: Crazy Horse and Wolf Tooth to the north, Lame White Man in the south, and Gall in the center. A portion of Gall's force, all mounted, stood off a short way to the south. Two Moon's small band – 180 men – occupied the Low Ridge southwest of Custer's position. Another 250 braves under Crow King held the rim of the ridge to the east of Keogh. The remaining 400 were far to the south, chasing Reno back to High Hill.

After more than an hour of furious maneuvers, Custer appeared curiously passive, making no move to rejoin Keogh or to break the encroaching encirclement. South Knoll also was fairly quiet, as it had been for some time, with the cavalrymen caught in a desultory, long-range crossfire.

Then, at 6:45, Two Moon inexplicably pulled his band back across the river.

Freed now to concentrate on a single enemy band, Custer seized the chance. At 6:51, *F Troop* begin a dismounted attack against North Hill. This effort was repulsed by a mixed bag of combatants under Wolf Tooth. In the meantime, though, *E Troop* rode down into the basin of the Greasy Grass southwest of the hill, successfully driving Gall's startled forces into the

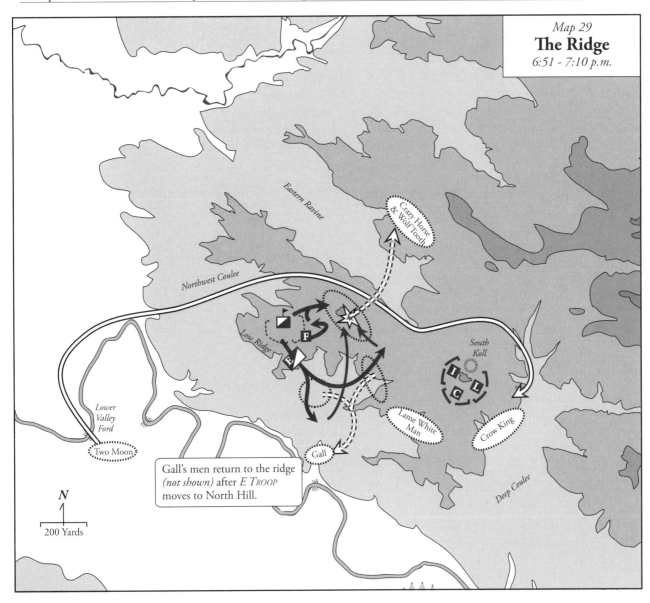

Map 29
The Ridge
6:51 - 7:10 p.m.

Gall's men return to the ridge *(not shown)* after *E TROOP* moves to North Hill.

N

200 Yards

nether regions of Deep Ravine. The troopers then split into platoons, with the *1ST* forming a mounted skirmish line, and the *2ND* going east toward the crest of the ridge. Dismounting, the troopers of *2ND PLATOON* swiftly advanced to the summit, bringing the Indians on North Hill within carbine range.

Indian resistance faded as *1ST PLATOON* reformed and charged north. Wolf Tooth watched as the enemy rode *"back toward a dry gulch, and following [its course] up the center of the basin, below where the monument now stands...and dismounted. The soldiers of the Gray Horse Troop got off their mounts and began to move up on foot."*

On the other side of the hill, *F TROOP* renewed its assault and, together with *1ST PLATOON / E TROOP*, converged toward the peak of the hill. The hostiles

promptly vacated, heading across Eastern Ravine. By 7:05 the entire spine of the Greasy Grass was firmly in the hands of the Custer battalion.

In the meantime, Two Moon's Cheyenne had regrouped. Riding across Lower Valley Ford, they headed through Northwest Coulee toward North Hill, in what almost certainly was a belated effort to support Crazy Horse and Wolf Tooth. Too late to do any good, Two Moon skirted past the soldiers, then swept south along the eastern slope of Greasy Grass Ridge, circling around South Knoll before coming to rest on Crow King's right in Deep Coulee.

As that occurred, Gall's following emerged to reoccupy the ground they had surrendered moments before. This left the men of *E TROOP'S 2ND PLATOON* exposed. *"The soldiers...took up three separate positions*

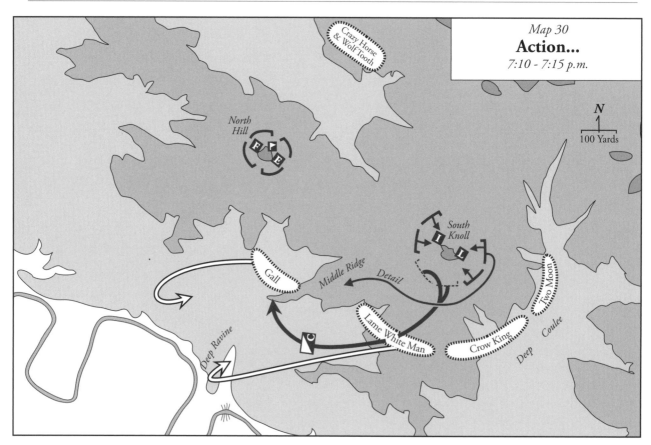

Map 30
Action...
7:10 - 7:15 p.m.

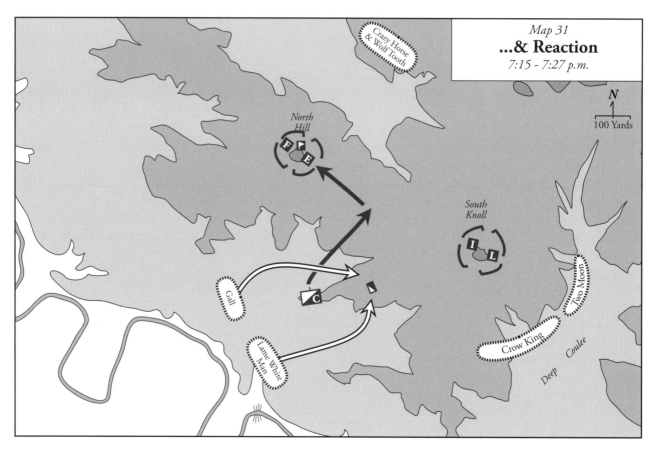

Map 31
...& Reaction
7:15 - 7:27 p.m.

along the ridge," said Ohiyesa, *"but were [still] practically hemmed in."* Remounting, they raced along the summit to rejoin their fellows on the hill.

Clearly, if Custer had wanted to reunite the portions of his command he easily could have done so. Why he did not is unknown, but it left Keogh in a bad situation. He could not have known what, if anything, Custer was planning. His men also were running low on ammunition, a shortage brought about in part from the loss of so many horses an hour earlier.

To reestablish contact, and to keep the enemy off balance, Keogh turned to Tom Custer's *LIGHT HORSE (C) TROOP,* the one company that had managed to retain almost all its animals. As seen by Kate Bighead, a Cheyenne and one of the first village noncombatants to cross the river: *"A line of soldiers on the ridge mounted their horses and came riding in a gallop down the broad coulee toward the river…The Indians…then got back quickly in[to] the deepest part of the gully [Deep Ravine], or kept on going away from it until they got over the ridge…where I was watching."*

In the action she referred to, *C TROOP* suddenly broke loose from its central position on the skirmish line. Sweeping first along the western shoulder of the ridge complex, they charged straight down into Greasy Grass Coulee, then circled right, up and onto Middle Ridge, stopping there at 7:15. In so doing they met little resistance from Gall and Lame White Man, both of whom simply got out of the way.

Three minutes later, a detachment of 10 men from *L TROOP* took position in the center of the ridge. Although they could provide cover, this move was yet another example of the pattern shown through Custer's command, of constantly dividing and redividing units rather than remaining concentrated.

With covering fire available, *C TROOP* moved off again, riding east onto the ridge top. They halted again, probably scrutinizing the western approaches for signs of Gall. The coast appeared clear, so the troop galloped on to Custer's strongpoint. Behind them, Lame White Man's Cheyenne moved to reclaim their former positions.

While *C TROOP* was moving, Keogh retracted his weakened lines by a third. In so doing he left Middle Ridge without mutually supporting fields of fire. The Indians were swift to take advantage of his error. Both Sioux and Cheyenne swept back into the vacated area, toward the now exposed *L TROOP* detail. Apparently unaware of their predicament, the troopers remained

in place, firing on the approaching enemy who dismounted just outside effective range. *"Within a few minutes there were many hundreds of warriors…along the gullies all around the soldiers,"* recalled Kate Bighead.

A brief but intense gunfight followed, related again by Kate: *"From where I was I had a clear view of the soldiers, and their saddled horses standing near them showed all the warriors where they were. I think only a few of the soldiers…were killed by the Indians during the few minutes of the fight there. I could not see enough of the crawling Indians to know if any one or another of them were killed."*

Remaining low, the tribesmen, in a coordinated effort, rapidly closed on the detachment. Within a short time most of the soldiers were at least wounded. Knowing the horrors that lay in store for anyone taken alive, many preferred suicide. *"They killed each other themselves,"* Cheyenne sub-chief Wooden Leg was later to state, *"all except four who tried to get away…on horseback. Unfortunately for them their animals were tired. Three of the men were quickly overtaken, while the fourth man — as the Sioux were going to overtake him — shot himself."*

***Captain Thomas W. Custer
Commanding C Troop, 7th Cavalry***

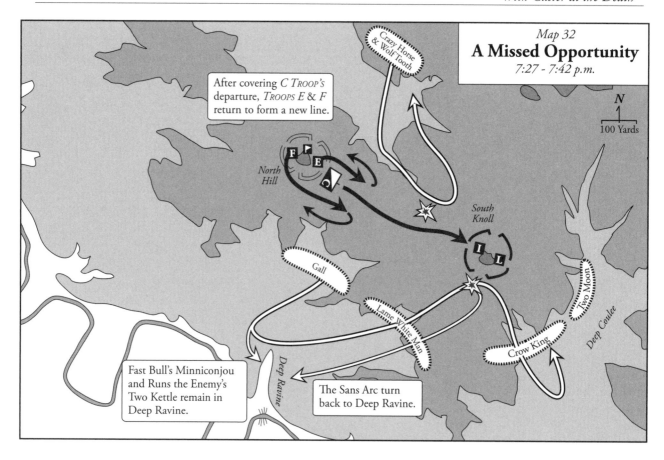

Map 32
A Missed Opportunity
7:27 - 7:42 p.m.

After covering *C Troop's* departure, *Troops E & F* return to form a new line.

North Hill

South Knoll

Gall

Deep Ravine

Fast Bull's Minniconjou and Runs the Enemy's Two Kettle remain in Deep Ravine.

The Sans Arc turn back to Deep Ravine.

Deep Coulee

N
100 Yards

It is probable Tom Custer was given all the saddlebag ammunition that could be spared. As he was preparing to head back toward South Knoll the men of his brother's command joined him. At 7:28 all three troops — *C Troop* in the center, with *E* and *F Troops* to the right and left, respectively — began moving out, leaving behind the headquarters detachment.

The drive came just too late to save the men of *L Troop*. Pushing along on a 300-yard front, the soldiers did not rush forward, but moved at a steady walk. After four minutes, having covered a third of the journey, they all dismounted. Smith and Yates remained in place, providing covering fire for *C Troop*.

The *Light Horse* carried on, now divided into three squads of seven men each. They continued their movement in a leapfrog fashion, with one squad moving at a time while the other two guarded its flanks. The Indians, taken aback by the coordinated movement, were unable to do anything until the advance had passed over the southern end of the ridge crest.

At about that time Crazy Horse struck, his braves firing as they came and cutting down three soldiers. *C Troop* was undeterred, arriving on South Knoll a few

minutes later. The ammunition was distributed, then the South Knoll position was realigned again, this time into a complete circle: *C Troop* on the west, *I Troop* on the southeast, and *L Troop* facing northeast.

Back at North Hill, *E* and *F Troops* had ceased firing once *C Troop* had passed out of range. Riding back several hundred yards, they dismounted and established a new battle line. Their horses were led back to the far side of the hill.

Down in Deep Ravine, Gall had grown tired of running from cavalry attacks on the exposed southern slope of Greasy Grass Ridge. He led his warriors out of the ravine, with Black Eagle's Sans Arc trailing behind.

Rather than returning to his original position, however, he chose a hazardous route eastward, up and over South Ridge. Keogh's troopers met the move with heavy fire. The Hunkpapa braved the fire to continue down the slope to link up with Two Moon and Crow King. The Sans Arc were unable to withstand the volleys; they turned back toward Deep Ravine, rejoining the handful of Two Kettle led by Runs The Enemy.

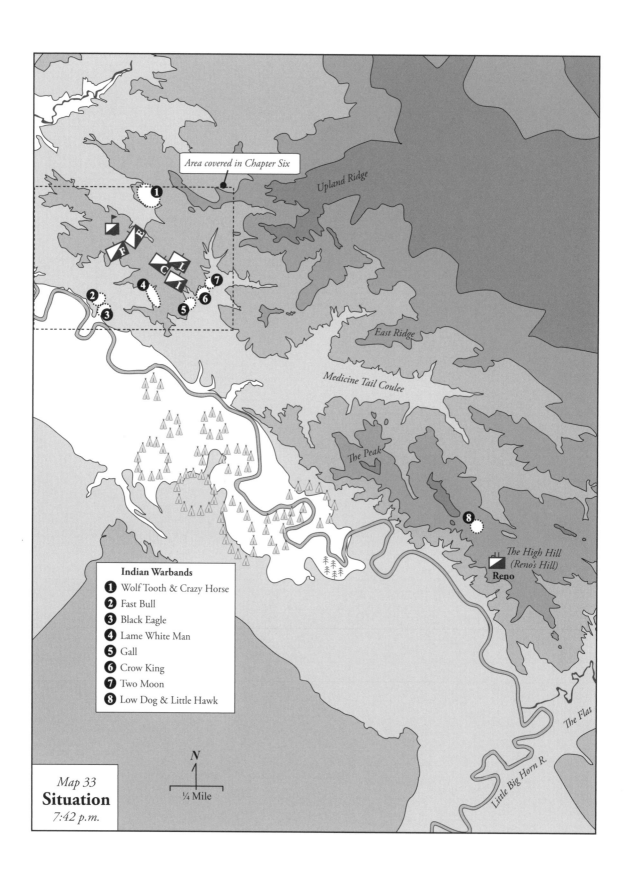

Area covered in Chapter Six

Upland Ridge

East Ridge

Medicine Tail Coulee

The Peak

The High Hill
(Reno's Hill)

Reno

Little Big Horn R.

The Flat

Indian Warbands

1. Wolf Tooth & Crazy Horse
2. Fast Bull
3. Black Eagle
4. Lame White Man
5. Gall
6. Crow King
7. Two Moon
8. Low Dog & Little Hawk

N

¼ Mile

Map 33
Situation
7:42 p.m.

Chapter Six
The South Knoll
7:42 p.m. - 8:34 p.m.

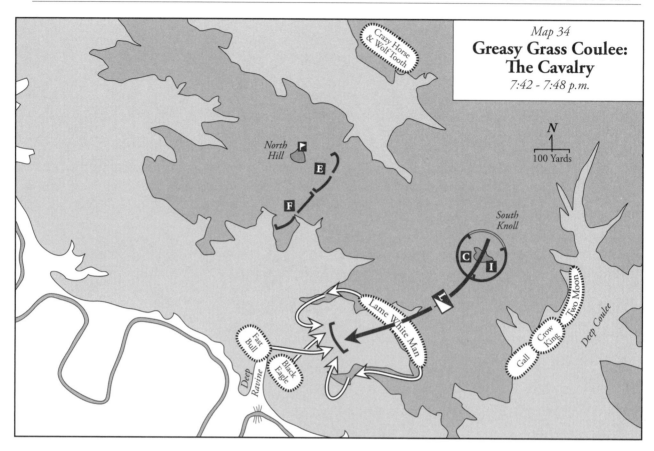

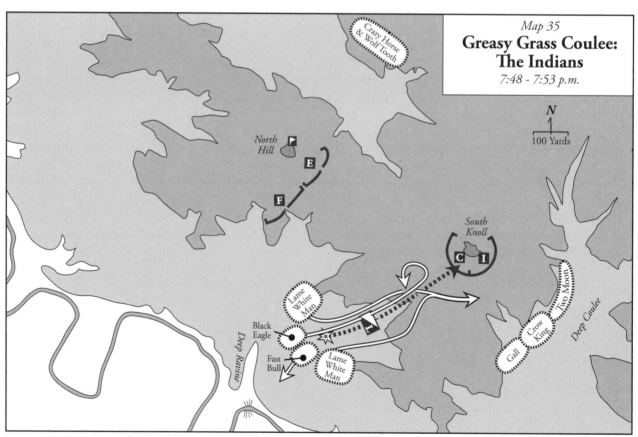

Gall's ride had a dramatic impact on the mind of Keogh, who decided to launch a counterattack just minutes after receiving the new supply of ammunition. Calhoun's *L Troop* moved across the strongpoint and pushed down Greasy Grass Coulee into the midst of the Agency Cheyenne. Once again, Lame White Man gave way rather than stand toe-to-toe with the troopers. The Minniconju sub-chief Red Horse remembered well that moment: *"One band of soldiers were right in the rear of us; when they charged we fell back and started firing at one another…We went back but a little distance when we spread out and encircled them."*

The men of *L Troop* got off their horses, setting up a new skirmish line. Red Horse continued: *"All this time we could see their officers out in front and hear them shouting to their men."*

Black Eagle's Sans Arc rode against the soldiers' western flank, followed by the dismounted Cheyenne: *"Then the Indians got courage and started for them in a solid body."*

The Indian attack was so fierce it forced Calhoun's front line back into the horse-holders, who already were having a difficult time. They held the beasts as tightly as they could, but to little avail. The result was chaotic for both sides as the unnerved animals began bucking, getting in everyone's way. Said Horned Horse:

"The smoke and dust were so thick that friend could not be distinguished from foe. "The horses were wild with fright and uncontrollable. The Indians were knocking each other over, and it is an absolute fact that [some of] the young braves, in their excitement and fury, killed each other. Some Indians were found killed by arrows."

The soldiers repelled the Indians, inflicting a substantial number of casualties. It was a small victory in the first close-encounter combat of the battle, and one the troopers had little time to enjoy. According to one of the braves there, the company *"held its ground for a time, but came under increasing fire from their left."*

Rather than remain pinned down, Calhoun beat a hasty retreat. Lame White Man recalled: *"The order to withdraw was given and the troops went for their horses. Only a few of them stopped to take careful aim. Most of the soldiers got up, ran forward, turned, fired and ran [again] — each soldier trying to get to his horse."*

While that was going on, Lame White Man rallied his own followers shouting in exultation: *"Come on! Now we can kill them all!"*

Against the new attack the troopers maintained a steady fire even as they pulled back. Three of their number were left behind and quickly were killed by the Minniconju. The Sans Arc, followed by the Agency Cheyenne, diligently pursued. Said one warrior: *"This was not a rout [but] a series of small retreats."*

The troopers mounted their horses, fired, rode a short distance, then turned about and fired again. The tribesmen kept coming at them through the whirling dust and confusion, and some of the soldiers were unhorsed. A total of four troopers fell along the way. One was hit just prior to reaching the South Knoll perimeter, and managed to scramble to safety. His associates were not so lucky. Two were killed outright; the third, his horse played out, was thrown to the ground. When he sprang to his feet he was quickly brought down again by a brave wielding a war club, then finished off with arrows as he tried to rise yet again. It was 7:53.

Nearly four miles to the south, the Brule under Little Hawk departed the site of the High Hill siege. It had been less than an hour since they had helped chase the forces of Maj. Reno and Capt. Benteen across

Lame White Man
War Chief of the (Agency) Cheyenne

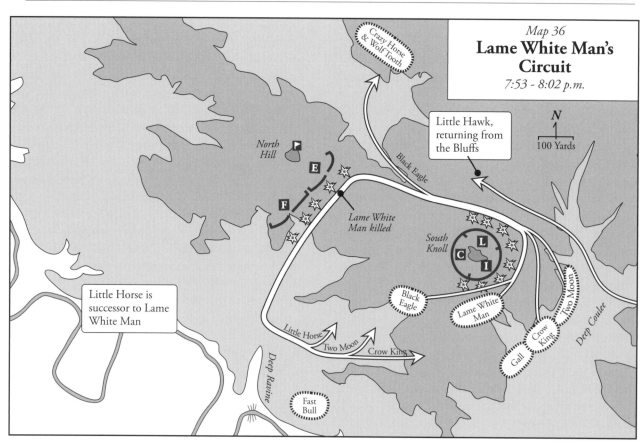

Map 36
Lame White Man's Circuit
7:53 - 8:02 p.m.

Little Hawk, returning from the Bluffs

Lame White Man killed

Little Horse is successor to Lame White Man

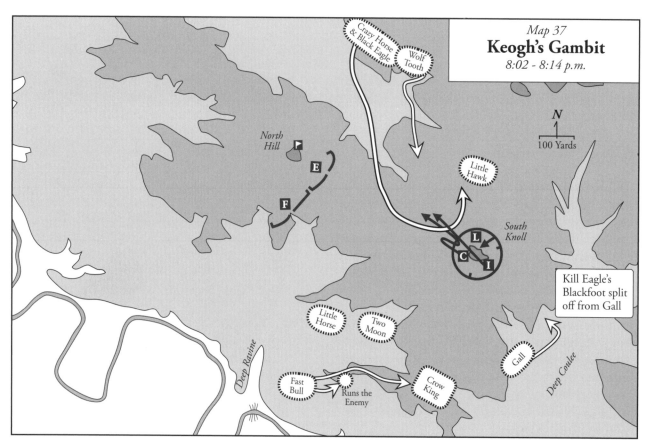

Map 37
Keogh's Gambit
8:02 - 8:14 p.m.

Kill Eagle's Blackfoot split off from Gall

the bluffs, away from any possibility of assisting Custer. Leaving the Agency Oglala of Low Dog in place, Little Hawk turned north, arriving atop the Peak and halting there momentarily. After observing what he could of the distant battlefield, he headed for an open range of land to the east of South Knoll, arriving there at 8:01.

In what appears to have been a spontaneous action, the Indians on the ridge began a circular sweep that pulled in most of the warriors in the vicinity. Lame White Man's Agency Cheyenne, this time trailed by the Sans Arc, coursed over South Ridge, then went east in a moving firefight with Keogh's troops. The warriors with Two Moon and Crow King leaped onto their ponies and followed close behind, arcing around the Knoll's south-eastern face, then north along the side of the ridge top. As the leading element of the Cheyenne surged toward the two companies deployed before North Hill, they were lashed by Custer's carbines. *Lame White Man charged at the south end…and all the way north…when he was killed,"* remembered Red Bird.

As the war chief fell – his place quickly taken by Little Horse – his column was forced to turn away toward Deep Ravine, running a fearful gauntlet of small arms fire from their right for a full minute. Black Eagle avoided that by edging to the right, down into and across the ravine to Eastern Ridge, there joining Crazy Horse and Wolf Tooth. Two Moon and Crow King followed in Lame White Man's wake. As the former recalled: *"I started back for the band of gray horses on the hill top…[but] I could not break the line and [so] went to the left…with the line of soldiers firing at me as I went."*

All three bands ended up where the great circuit had begun 10 minutes earlier, in Greasy Grass Coulee.

Even as the Sioux and Cheyenne were completing their ride, *C Troop* began a diversionary effort at 8:03, shifting its left wing behind the right, then moving about 50 yards beyond the perimeter. After firing a few shots, the troopers reversed direction, arriving back at their start line three minutes later. The ruse worked. With the Indians distracted, *I* and *L Troops* fell back. The soldiers, said Gall, moved at the double to reach their horses on the Knoll. The Blackfoot quickly followed, closing the range to improve their accuracy.

Once its brother companies were in place, the *Light Horse Troop* again headed north a full 300 yards. *"The second time they moved forward they did not turn back,"* said Flying Hawk, but finally *"halted and made another stand before they fled."*

Seeing the puzzling actions, the warriors with Crazy Horse wanted to strike immediately. He refused, however, content to observe with dispassionate deliberation. Then the less patient Sans Arc took things into their own hands by initiating a daring run, with the sub-chief White Bull leading the way. Riding up Eastern Ravine, then along the slope of Greasy Grass ridge top, they made a sharp turn east through the gap between *C Troop* and the bluecoats on South Knoll, arriving at Little Hawk's location followed by a reluctant Crazy Horse. The Wolf Tooth group, however, simply moved along Eastern Ridge to occupy a hill several hundred yards to the north of their allies.

Whatever Keogh might have thought of those counter-moves, he hardly had time to deliberate. Just after the *Light Horse Troop* moved out, the men on the Knoll were dealt another blow. As bugles sounded and the men of *I* and *L Troops* attempted to mount up, the Hunkpapa and Blackfoot unleashed a torrent of arrows on them. At first one or two horses broke away in terror; the fear spread until it affected the majority of the mounts, which scattered in all directions. As witnessed by Kate Bighead, who by that time had made her way around the battle area to the east of Keogh: *"Each arrow was shot far upward and forward…to curve down and fall where they were…a rain of arrows from thousands of Indian bows, and kept up for a long time would hit many soldiers."*

With an effective range of just 50 yards, it is doubtful the arrows did much harm, though there was a psychological impact. It appeared to the Indians their arrow barrage came as an unexpected shock to their opponents, causing the captain to hasten his departure before all was genuinely ready. It seems he and his men were on the verge of panic after enduring about four minutes of the horrific downpour, and he promptly ordered *I Troop* to lead the way north. From his location to the southwest, Gall had seen the effect the arrows were having, and correctly guessed the soldiers were about to abandon the hill. As he prepared to attack, the Keogh command got on the move, with Lt. Calhoun's company taking over as rear guard.

At about 8:15, Gall launched his charge just as Keogh reached *C Troop* at the head of Eastern Ravine. Letting loose with the piercingly shrill screech of eagle-bone whistles, which cut through the noise of the fighting, the Hunkpapa surged forward while Kill Eagle's dismounted Blackfoot rose up and followed. Those on horseback came on like a tidal wave that washed over

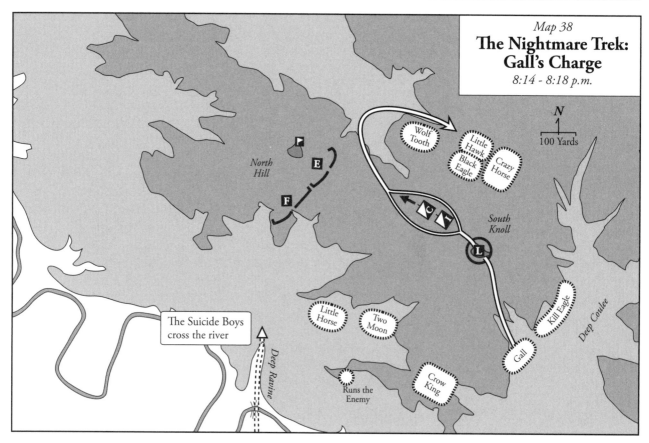

Map 38
**The Nightmare Trek:
Gall's Charge**
8:14 - 8:18 p.m.

the Calhoun position. *L Troop's* remaining 31 men fell victim to the Indians, who cut them down before they could organize a final stand. Gall had the impression he had crushed all the resistance on the Knoll: *"Finally we charged through them with our ponies. When we had done this…the fight was over."*

Actually, it was not quite finished. For though badly mauled, the cavalrymen were still intact as a unit and able to turn their weapons against Kill Eagle's second wave. The Blackfoot gave a war whoop and rushed forward, eager to come to grips with the enemy. Their sweep stopped in an instant as Calhoun's men unleashed a diminished but still potent volley. That forced a rapid retreat of the Blackfoot even as Gall and his warriors continued on their way.

Keogh and his men could see what was happening behind them, but were in no position to do anything about it. Knowing they would be next, *C* and *I Troops* departed in haste. *"A bugle blew and those soldiers who still had horses remounted,"* said White Bull. *"After all the troops combined together, they began to move north again in a single body."*

Passing down the north slope of the Knoll, the Hunkpapa slammed into the rear of the column. Nine of Keogh's remaining 41 men were cut off in the new

onslaught and had to be left behind. Those men, Gall remarked, *"never broke, but retreated step by step…[until] they were shot down where they stood."*

The Indians split into two streams, which first enveloped then bypassed the troopers. As the hostiles merged again, they glided right, avoiding Custer's line, riding across the Eastern Ravine, then up toward the hill just vacated by Wolf Tooth and Crazy Horse.

Keogh was not out of danger yet. Wolf Tooth had foreseen his line of march and advanced his band into the head of the ravine. After the front of the column passed, the warriors opened up with a galling fire.

At least 26 of the remaining 32 members of Keogh's column were still in the saddle. They kept going without pause, for anything less meant certain annihilation. Getting to North Hill was their only thought, their only hope. Though the gathering dusk reduced them to fleeting shadows, men in blue were still intermittently dropping along the way.

For Calhoun's men atop South Knoll — minus their now-deceased commander — things were no less grim. Mangled and isolated, they faced dismounted warriors to the south, mounted ones to the east and west. The remnant of *L Troop* found a last refuge behind the irregular semi-circle of 18 dead horses – only one animal was still on its feet at the Knoll – set up earlier in the fight.

Over on North Hill, Custer's men were holding the line facing east, keeping open a gateway for Keogh. *"At first the general kept his men intact,"* said Ohiyesa, *"and fired volley after volley at the whirling enemy."*

While Custer watched, Runs The Enemy, war chief of the Two Kettle, looked to the west. He noticed the vulnerable position of Custer's horses a few hundred yards behind the firing line, next to the headquarters detachment. Seeing a chance to scatter the animals, he made his way down West Ridge toward the river, leaving behind most of his followers. He signaled to a group of under-aged youths, most of them Cheyenne, known as the "Suicide Boys." They were self-appointed village guardians who had sworn a sacred oath to defend their people to the death and to undertake without question any assignment given them.

Starting out near Deep Ravine Ford, the youths rode forward just as Gall was about to strike South Knoll. As Runs The Enemy later described it: *"I left my men and rushed around the hills, and came up to the north end of the field…From the point that juts out below where the monument now stands, about 30 of us got through the lines and captured a lot of Custer's horses."*

Moving rapidly through the ravine, then on toward North Hill, they got behind the general's exposed western flank undetected. Heading toward the crest of the hill, the Indians were suddenly in the midst of the astonished horse-holders.

"The deafening war whoops and the rattling sound of gun shots frightened the horses," recalled Ohiyesa. The troopers lost control of a large number of the animals, which were spooked to run past the headquarters detachment and through the *F Troop* area, knocking men aside as they went. Too late, the soldiers opened fire on the raiders, who turned toward the head of Keogh's column, which just had passed over the spine of the ridge.

The riders of *C Troop* found their retreat temporarily slowing to a halt as they tried to avoid colliding with the onrushing swarm of horses, which careened through and around their column, driven relentlessly by Runs The Enemy's brazen bunch.

Though the troopers managed to kill two of the Suicide Boys, the youths and their older companions had already done their damage. They went on, passing swiftly down Greasy Grass Coulee to its mouth, then in

the direction of Deep Ravine Ford, finally driving the horses into the adjoining village wickiup area.

Keogh's situation went from bad to worse without a respite. Crazy Horse now descended on him from the right, bisecting the column at a point south of the ridge crest. In the words of He Dog, the charge *"broke through and split the soldiers into two bunches."* Crazy Horse continued down the west side of Greasy Grass Ridge to Deep Ravine, pulling up beside the groups of Two Moon and Little Hawk.

On Crazy Horse's right, Black Eagle and his Sans Arc attempted to block *C Troop*, but were too close to Custer's field of fire. Determined nevertheless to harass the enemy and keep the two commands from reuniting, they remained behind and to the east of Keogh.

I Troop was stranded and Tom Custer's spearhead was on the verge of disintegrating. According to one of the Oglala sub-chiefs, Foolish Elk, *"the men on horseback rode away just as fast as they could."* It was a full-fledged rout likened by witnesses to a "stampede of buffalo." Capt. Custer made it to his older brother's lines with just 20 of his men. Looking around hopelessly, they

First Lieutenant James Calhoun Commanding L Troop, 7th Cavalry

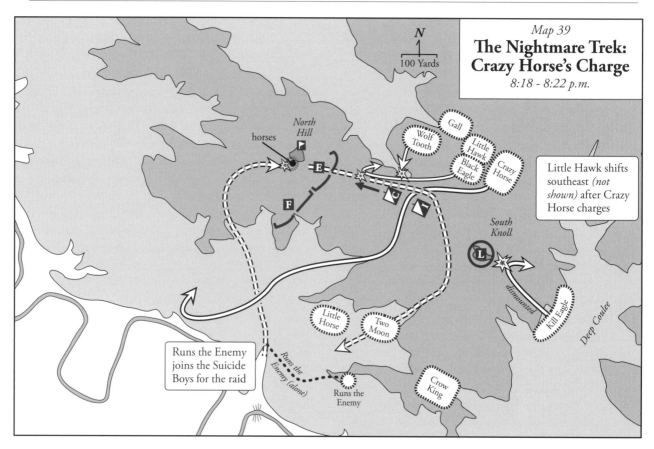

Little Hawk shifts southeast *(not shown)* after Crazy Horse charges

Runs the Enemy joins the Suicide Boys for the raid

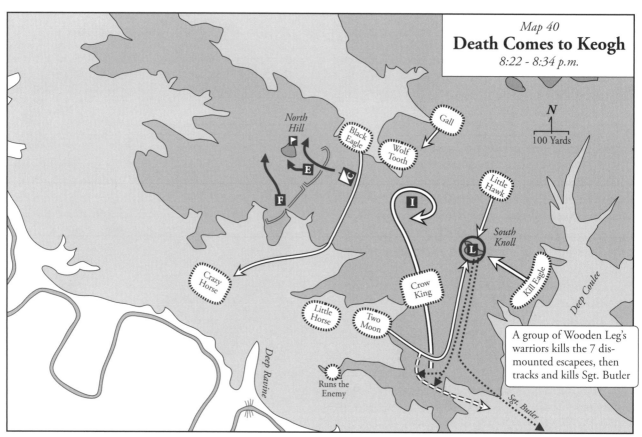

A group of Wooden Leg's warriors kills the 7 dismounted escapees, then tracks and kills Sgt. Butler

could only see swirling eddies of dust being thrown up by the Hunkpapa of Crow King, who wasted little time encircling the surviving remnant of Myles Keogh's command, a dozen men at most.

The soldiers with Keogh, several of them still on horseback, quickly consolidated, but the Indians were relentless. The Sans Arc fired on them from the east while Crow King came on them from the west. That chief remembered: *"They were all drawn up in a line of battle, shooting well and fighting hard, but there were so many [of our] people around them they could not help being killed. They…kept fighting and falling from their horses — fighting and falling all the way."*

One by one all the remaining horses went down, until all the men were left afoot. Keogh himself had his left knee shattered by the same bullet that passed through the body of his mount.

Crow King made an unsuccessful effort to overrun them but, obliged to turn around, the Hunkpapa then opted for an encirclement that finally forced the column to stop on the eastern slope of Greasy Grass Ridge. With that accomplished, the Sans Arc considered their work done and rode off to rejoin Crazy Horse.

The spirited bluecoat commander and his remaining handful were still unbroken and defiant despite a noticeable drop in their fire According to Red Feather, he and his comrades *"got the idea the[ir]… guns were empty, and [so] charged immediately on the soldiers."*

The Indians repeatedly sliced through Keogh's line to close in and around the soldiers *"like intertwining fingers,"* according to Horned Horse. There was soon such a mix of combatants the Wolf Tooth group stopped firing for fear of hitting their fellow braves.

Things became so close that the troopers who still had ammunition had no time to reload. They discarded their carbines and began firing at pointblank range with pistols. Nearly out of ammunition, they clustered into five small groups and, from all accounts, faced their end with resignation and courage. The Sioux and Cheyenne present referred to this last massing as *"little knots of soldiers"* who fought with momentary brilliance before they were *"ground up"* by the overwhelming numbers they faced. It was later reported Keogh's last few troopers made a considerable fight of it, and a large number of warriors became casualties as a result. One Indian noted: *"The soldiers seemed tired, but they fought to the end."*

That was how it ended for Keogh, who, together with First Sergeant Frank Varden of *I Troop*, resisted to the last. The two men, one standing, the other kneeling, completely alone, pumped out the last rounds in their weapons against the final, massed charge that then trampled them underfoot.

As the Keogh command was being wiped out, equally tragic events were about to take place on South Knoll. Exactly how many of the original 31 men on the summit were still in fighting shape is unknown, but there were enough to force Kill Eagle's men to remain under cover and at a distance. The surviving troopers could have no illusions about their pending fate. Realizing that, one of them, First Sergeant James Butler of *L Troop*, mounted the last upright horse and somehow managed to skirt past the enemy toward the southwest. It was 8:25 p.m.

Moments later the gunfire faded to a few scattered shots. After a time even that ceased and silence enveloped the hilltop. *"The white men are all dead!"* Kate Bighead remembered shouting. *"The shots quit coming from the place where the soldiers were lying behind the dead horses. All the Indians jumped up and ran toward them, supposing them all dead. But there were seven white men who sprang to their feet and went running toward the river."*

With the Indians rushing on them, the seven attempted to follow Butler's lead. They do not appear to have been aware of the presence of two large groups of warriors, the Agency and Non-Agency Cheyenne of Little Horse and Two Moon, who still occupied Greasy Grass Coulee. A group of the Non-Agency Cheyenne, led by sub-chief Wooden Leg, intercepted and killed some of them. A second contingent of mounted braves got the rest a minute later with lance and tomahawk, then went after Butler.

After a mile-long chase, they saw their quarry's horse stumble. Butler managed to unsling his carbine and open fires even as he tried to make his way on foot. He finally fell, shot down from a distance, with his newly-reloaded pistol still spewing death.

An anti-climactic denouement took place atop the Knoll. Kill Eagle's Blackfoot were heading rapidly toward the rise, soon to be joined by Little Hawk's Brule and the bulk of Wooden Leg's party. The Indians encountered little resistance from the few soldiers still alive on the ground, and slaughtered them all. At about 8:34 p.m., four hours after its initial occupation, South Knoll was back in Indian hands. All that remained to be done was wipe out the 100 or so *Wasichus* (whites) who still held the opposite end of the ridge.

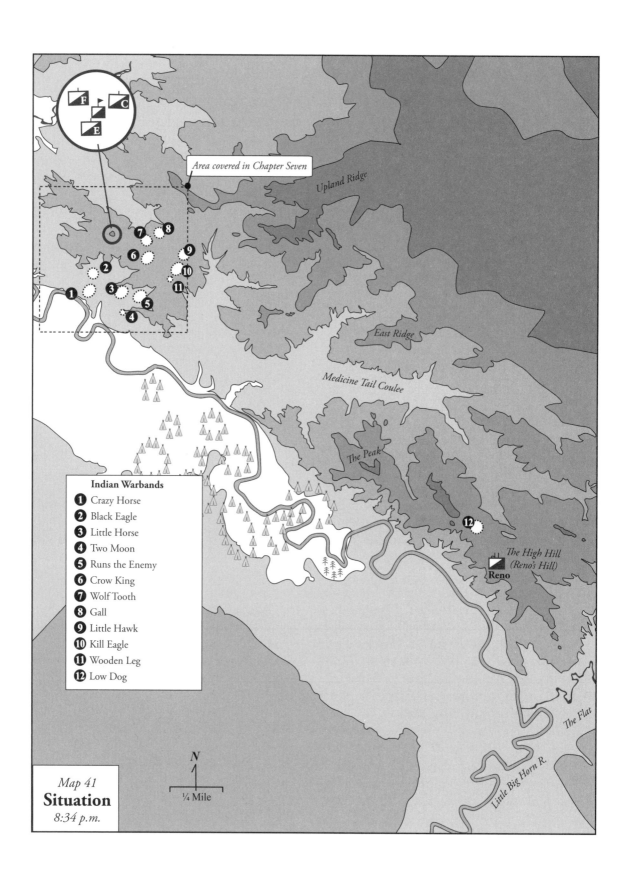

Indian Warbands

1. Crazy Horse
2. Black Eagle
3. Little Horse
4. Two Moon
5. Runs the Enemy
6. Crow King
7. Wolf Tooth
8. Gall
9. Little Hawk
10. Kill Eagle
11. Wooden Leg
12. Low Dog

Area covered in Chapter Seven

Upland Ridge

East Ridge

Medicine Tail Coulee

The Peak

The High Hill
(Reno's Hill)

Reno

Little Big Horn R.

The Flat

N

¼ Mile

Map 41
Situation
8:34 p.m.

The Last Stand
8:34 p.m. -9:54 p.m.

Powerless to intervene in the catastrophic events that overtook Keogh, Custer concentrated on trying to salvage what was left of his battalion. This amounted to no more than 103 men, fewer than half those he had brought across North Fork Creek that afternoon.

Even before the Indians finished their bloody work to the south, the general began a two-phased withdrawal to North Hill. The Minniconju brave named Lights observed: *"At that point each company would alternate in covering the retreat of the other."*

Custer placed the men into a circular line that extended just 85 yards beyond the summit. His brother's troops were stationed along the northeast quadrant; Lt. Smith's *E Troop* occupied the southern sector; and Yates' *F Troop* held the northwest. In the center, at the crest of the hill, a barricade of horse carcasses roughly 10-by-15 yards across, protected the field headquarters and medical aid station. Directly adjacent to it on the upper western slope, as before, were gathered the command's remaining mounts. Custer, a distinctive red bandana around his neck, stationed himself within the barricade. By 8:32 he and his battalion were as ready as they could be. According to Two Moon the bluecoats formed a double line to meet the anticipated onslaught: *"Some of the soldiers were down on their knees; some were standing, officers all in front."*

The tribal bands did not begin to advance again until the last resistance elsewhere had been snuffed out with absolute certainty. *"The country was alive with Indians going in all directions,"* said one Oglala, *"like myriads of swallows, yet the great body [of them] all the time moving down on Custer."*

What took shape was a massive convergence of most of the remaining warriors in the area of the Greasy Grass ridge top at 8:36. As related by Two Moon: *"The greater portion of our warriors came together in front, and .. we turned our horses against [the whites]."*

He also claimed there was some talk of trying to simply overrun Custer's position. Crazy Horse remarked they were dealing with a still-formidable opponent. He suggested an encircling maneuver that might soften up the North Hill bastion before any head-on assault. In his plan the various bands would maneuver around to the east and west of the hill while he returned to his own group to remain in place with them until the start of the final attack. With the troopers' attentions already distracted, the Oglala would vacate Deep Ravine to move as covertly as possible into a new location from which to strike directly into the enemy.

The idea was unanimously accepted and the conference broke up. Within another minute the operation was underway. The Sioux went up to the right, the Cheyenne to the left. *"Warriors rode out on each side of them and circled them until they were surrounded,"* said Two Moon. As that was happening, the Sans Arc galloped to the top of Middle Ridge.

By 8:41 the Indian redeployment was complete, and an instant later they charged up the slopes toward Custer's position. The general's men immediately opened fire, but the onrushing Indians did not waver. Only at the last minute, with just 50 yards to go, they all turned to the right to start the first of five runs around the strongpoint. Each circuit lasted just two minutes, with both sides throwing out a ceaseless flow of bullets. One of those hit at the outset of this phase was a Sioux leader named Hump: *"In the first charge the Indians never slackened or stopped…My horse was shot from under me, and I was wounded — shot above the knee and the bullet came out at the hip, and I fell and lay right there. The other Indians kept going."*

Everyone on North Hill was within rifle range. Those on horseback were particularly vulnerable. The majority of the soldiers in the strongpoint took up prone positions, rather than continue to stand or kneel. *"Falling on the ground,"* said Ohiyesa, *"they sent volley after volley into the whirling masses of the enemy."*

According to the Arapahoe brave named Waterman: *"There was a great deal of noise and confusion. The air was heavy with powder smoke, and the Indians were yelling. The Indians on horseback had shields and rode on the sides of their ponies so the soldiers could not hit them. The soldiers were entirely surrounded, and the whole countryside was alive with Indians…thousands of them!"*

A 15-year-old Sioux spectator recalled: *"It reminded me of a whole flock of magpies swirling around a hill, going 'round and 'round.'"*

Said Two Moon: *"We shoot! We ride fast! We shoot again! Soldiers in line drop! But one man rides up and down, all the time shouting. I do not know who he was. He was a brave man."*

Custer's horse-holders, of necessity reduced to a minimum, were having a hard time of it. One soldier led eight to 10 horses, and as conditions worsened the mounts became unmanageable, finally breaking free. *"The last we could see from our side of the river,"* said Pretty White Buffalo, *"was a great number of scattering gray horses. The smoke and shooting and the dust of the horses shot out of the hill, and the soldiers fired many shots, but the Sioux shot straight."*

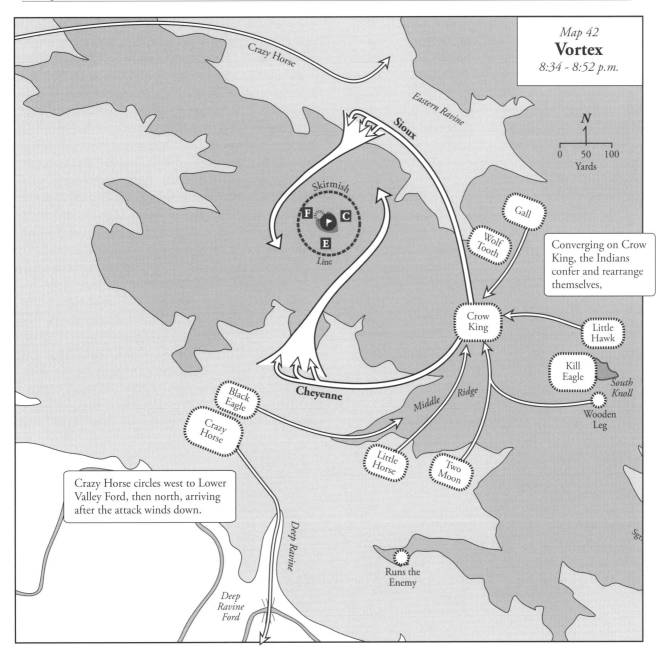

The warriors never let up the pressure. *"We circled around them, swirling like water around a stone,"* said Two Moon. *"The Indians kept swirling 'round and 'round, and the soldiers killed a few...Once in a while some man would break out and run toward the river, but he would fall...All along the bugler kept blowing commands. He was brave too. Then the chief was killed. I heard it was Long Hair [but] I don't know."*

Indeed, it probably was at that moment George Armstrong Custer died. Hit in the side by a long-range shot, Custer sank to the ground, eyes closed, hands still grasping his rifle, finger still on the trigger. His men, still firing, probably did not see him fall.

The circling attacks came to an end after about 10 minutes. As Crazy Horse arrived in position, the Sioux under Gall retired once again just beyond the crest of the ridge. Two Moon's Non-Agency Cheyenne went north and halted about a third of a mile from North Hill, taking up station on Far Ridge. The Agency Cheyenne, led by Little Horse, continued west across Low Ridge and down into the Basin.

Not all the Indians were involved in the fighting. The Two Kettle and Wolf Tooth's group remained in place, while Kill Eagle's Blackfoot moved from South Knoll to Middle Ridge, joining the Sans Arc.

Crazy Horse made a longer ride. Leading his Oglala south over Deep Ravine Ford, he met the Suicide Boys *en route*. Soon after, the youths — having been instructed to remain nearby — diverged toward Greasy Grass Ford and stopped there. Crazy Horse continued riding, leading his band back across the river at Lower Valley Ford. From there, the Oglala coursed north, arriving in Eastern Ravine. By 8:52, they pulled up at a point about 600 yards from North Hill just as the fifth and final circuit was being completed.

Though the warriors had their enemies surrounded, there was a lull, as if all were pausing to catch their breath. It appears the surviving cavalry officers

— probably Capt. Yates and Lts. Cooke, Harrington, Reiley, and Smith — believed the existing line was no longer tenable; so they ordered one last retreat. It was then they learned, to their undoubted shock, that both the general and his brother Tom were dead. It was also only then they found almost all the horse-holders had been either killed or wounded, though a fair number of free mounts still roamed the hilltop. Even the Indians saw it. *"By this time,"* said Wolf Tooth, *"[the horses] were mainly loose — the ones that had not been shot."*

The troopers made a hurried effort to recapture some horses, but the frightened animals took off in every direction, all but a handful escaping into the surrounding countryside. That prompted a diversion of

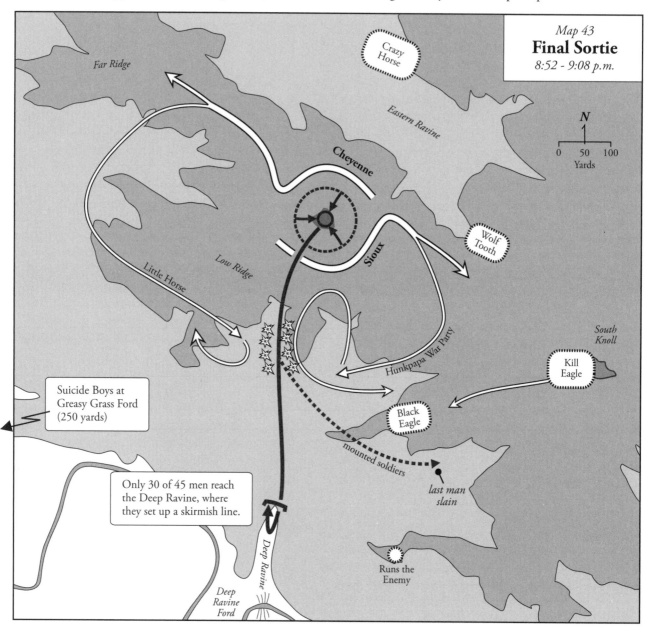

Map 43
Final Sortie
8:52 - 9:08 p.m.

Far Ridge

Crazy Horse

Eastern Ravine

N
0   50   100
Yards

Cheyenne

Little Horse

Low Ridge

Sioux

Wolf Tooth

South Knoll

Hunkpapa War Party

Kill Eagle

Suicide Boys at Greasy Grass Ford (250 yards)

Black Eagle

Only 30 of 45 men reach the Deep Ravine, where they set up a skirmish line.

mounted soldiers

last man slain

Deep Ravine

Runs the Enemy

Deep Ravine Ford

Indian strength, as many braves turned to chase the valuable creatures. Some had the impression the horses had been let go deliberately.

Not all the horses were on the run. At least 33 mounts had been slain during the recent fighting, or were so seriously crippled they had to be shot. The carcasses were dragged into a new barricade on the western slope. The makeshift parapet — essentially an outer ring surrounding the existing headquarters ring — gave the men an expanded berm roughly 30 yards in diameter. "*The remaining soldiers were keeping themselves behind their dead horses,*" remembered Kate Bighead.

To the Indians, who had crept forward to renew their earlier sniping, it was clear the whites were far from broken. They still had weapons and a seemingly plentiful supply of ammunition. For a short time a siege ensued, similar to the earlier one on South Knoll.

Wolf Tooth recalled there would be "*furious bursts of gunfire*" from North Hill as the combat temporarily reverted to longer-range shooting: "*The soldier would aim carefully, and he was more likely to hit you.*" So the warriors again were forced to take cover, while a thick gray haze of gunsmoke began to fill the nearly motionless air.

Among the surrounded bluecoats it was decided to try to breakout toward the river. Half the remaining men, about 45 of them including several civilians and a large portion of *E Troop*, were picked or volunteered for the undertaking. They apparently would be led by one of the few remaining able-bodied officers, Lt. Henry M. Harrington of the *Light Horse Troop*. At 9:02 that party, only seven of them mounted, began their hazardous journey with a bugle call.

"*At the command the soldiers rose up in unison and headed downhill toward the river in the direction of a small ravine,*" said Wooden Leg. "*[A] man on a sorrel horse led them, shouting all the time. He wore a buckskin shirt and had long black hair and a moustache...His men were all covered with dust.*"

Seeing them emerge, the Indians let go a cry of warning. The would-be escapees' objective was the head of Deep Ravine, a distance of just over a half-mile. They made every effort to keep order and thereby stop their natural fears from expanding into panic. Most reportedly kept their head as they rushed forward as fast as they could, but others proved unable to keep the pace and began to straggle farther and farther behind.

Of course, by that time many of the troopers were exhausted, mentally and physically drained, bewildered and frightened. They almost surely were running out of both water and ammunition — and hope. In the terrible heat their sweat-soaked, dirt-encrusted clothing was heavy, and even their weapons must have seemed unwieldy. Several of them discarded their carbines almost as soon as they moved out; others retained their rifles without using them, preferring to fire their pistols instead. As Sitting Bull stated: "*They were brave men, but they were too tired...they could not stand firmly on their feet. They swung to and fro...like the limbs of a cypress in a great wind. Some of them struggled under the weight of their guns.*"

For the first time in the battle, the Indians did not retreat in the face of a cavalry advance. "*Instead of giving way,*" recalled Two Moon, "*the Cheyenne met the rush with hot lead and a...charge.*" The Hunkpapa remounted and raced off to the right, coming around and behind the troopers. The maneuver had a devastating impact on those in the back half of the column. In short order, the rear-most 10 men fell, including Boston Custer and Autie Reed, brother and nephew of the general.

As the Indians closed in, many of the escapees became disoriented. "*The soldiers who were killed were horsemen,*" said Sitting Bull, "*but they had no chance to fight or run away; they were surrounded too closely by our many warriors. As they stood there waiting to be killed, they were seen to look far away to the hills in all directions; and we knew they were looking for the hidden soldiers in the hollow of the hills to come and help them.*"

Iron Hawk, a Sioux brave, stated: "*When they saw the soldiers running down...the Hunkpapa rode right up to the soldiers and encircled them,*" close enough "*to look them in the eyes.*"

When confronted that way some of the troopers continued to fight, but others became so terrified they fainted or froze. "*Some of the men were wearing hand revolvers in their belts that were never used. Custer's men, in the beginning, shot straight, but later shot like drunken men, firing into the ground, into the air, wildly in every way,*" recalled another combatant, Lying Down. "*The warriors were taking the guns away from the soldiers. Also, the soldiers, in running away became so demoralized they would fire their guns in the air, and made themselves easy victims when caught.*" Thus many at the tail end of the breakout party ended up, according to White Bull, running "*like scared rabbits.*"

For those in front, though, it was different. They made it through the Indian lines in front of Deep Ravine, but then the endless harassment made them alter

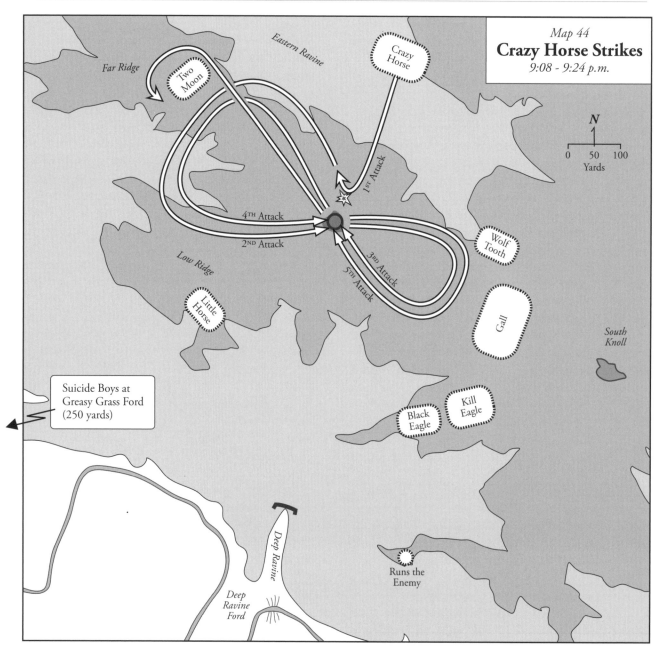

their route. They turned down toward a smaller coulee, while those on horseback (two of whom already had fallen) tried to ride off toward Reno. They were soon brought down by small arms fire on the western slopes of Middle Ridge, while those afoot tried to press on toward Deep Ravine. Good Voiced Elk remembered they *"jumped over the steep bank into the gully,"* where they turned around and set up a defense across the irregular terrain. There were only 30 still alive.

After some delay, Crazy Horse led his followers across Eastern Ravine at 9:09, in what turned into a series of mounted assaults on the North Hill position.

As Ohiyesa related: *"The signal was given for a general charge. Crazy Horse and the Oglala...now came forward with a tremendous yell."*

When the Indians emerged over a nearby rise they were met by a blast of gunfire that threw them off balance. Ohiyesa continued: *"The brave soldiers sent a large volley into their ranks, which shocked them for a time. At that moment a soldier on a swift horse struck for the river but was brought down."*

The failure of their initial rush forced the Oglala to move north, toward Two Moon, then loop around in a wide arc to launch a second effort. They charged full-tilt against the western perimeter, where the soldiers quickly gathered, and again the roar of their carbines was heard. Though still powerful, their firepower was no longer strong enough to stop the hostiles. That time the war ponies broke across the top of the redoubt, then rode through it.

To those watching the onslaught it was hard to imagine anyone could survive such an attack. The cavalrymen were soon visible, though, moving toward the southern half of the barricade to face the next assault.

Crazy Horse had known from the start it would take repeated runs to achieve success, and he led his braves in a figure-eight pattern centered on the redoubt. Third, fourth and fifth charges were made, the mounted warriors surging forward again and again and again. According to Wolf Tooth, though, each time the bluecoats would *"turn from side to side"* and fire their weapons. Though the charges looked formidable, and no doubt would have been on a stretch of open prairie, here they did not achieve their intended effect: the defenders' fire could not be silenced.

This was because of the protection provided by the inner and outer rings of dead horses, enabling the troopers to avoid being trampled. They kept as close as possible to the carcasses, waiting until the Indians came within easy range, then loosed fusillades into them at the last second. Dropping to the ground to avoid the horse, they left open the center of the strongpoint. The

Crazy Horse
War Chief of the (Non-Agency) Oglala

An Indian painting of the battle. The "Last Stand" is at the upper left.

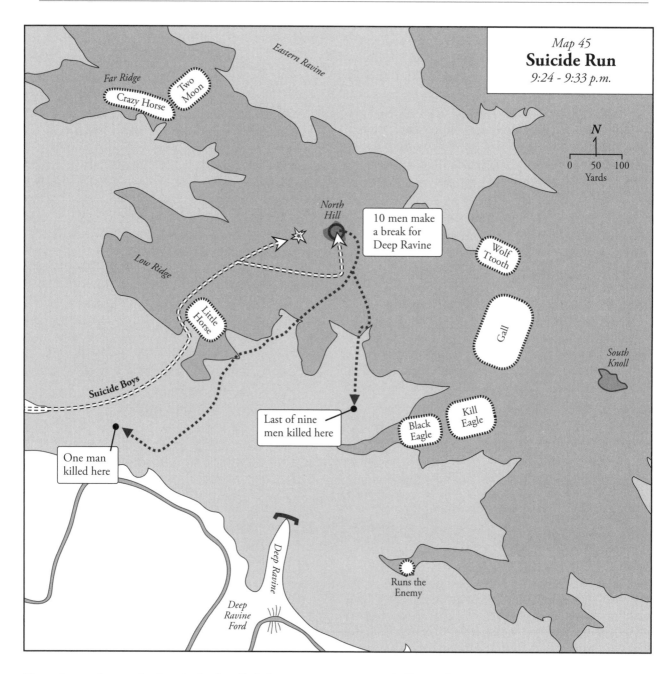

Map 45
Suicide Run
9:24 - 9:33 p.m.

Sioux jumped over the barricade, hurdled the opposite side, and made their exit. They inflicted only little damage on the defenders. After about a minute, approximately the time it took each charge to completely pass, the soldiers would rise up, reload, then turn once again to wait for their foe to return.

At 9:24, following the fifth charge, Crazy Horse pulled up to the right of Two Moon on Far Ridge. Looking toward North Hill, he was exasperated to find his efforts were in vain. Something had to be done quickly: many Indians were running low on ammuni-

tion – Gall's Hunkpapa in particular had used all their cartridges – and in just a half-hour it would be completely dark. It seemed there was only one alternative left: an all-out, hand-to-hand, head-on assault, delivered simultaneously from every side. It was something Crazy Horse had hoped to avoid, but he dispatched a rider to the Suicide Boys, still at Greasy Grass Ford. They would lead the final effort.

Just then a group of 10 whites jumped to their feet and began running down the south slope toward the river. Though obstructed only by the Sans Arc sub-chief, White Bull, and four other braves, the fleeing men quickly became the targets of other nearby tribesmen. *"Two soldiers were in the lead,"* recalled White Bull, *"one of them wounded and bleeding from the mouth."*

When they got near, the sub-chief and a companion shot two of them, then ran over to count coup (touch the bodies). All but one of the other troopers took advantage of the Indians' distraction to run by, only to be overtaken and killed by other hostiles. There soon remained only a single survivor, who headed west. As witnessed by Two Moon, *"that man, alone, ran far down toward the river, then 'round a hill. I thought he was going to make it, but a Sioux fired and hit him in the head. He was the last man. He had stripes on his arms."*

It was 9:31. and the Suicide Boys were riding up North Hill. With the battle reaching its climax, the boys were just the thing the Indians needed to finish it. It was Crazy Horse who made the final decision to commit them to the fight. Remembered Wolf Tooth:

> *"Before long some Sioux came along behind the horses and began calling in the Sioux language to get ready and watch the Suicide Boys. They were getting ready down below to charge together from the river, and when they came in, all the Indians up above should jump up for hand-to-hand fighting. That way the soldiers would not have a chance to shoot, but would be crowded from both sides…The criers called out these instructions several times. Most of the Cheyenne could not understand this, and [others of] the Sioux then told us what they had said."*

The Suicide Boys, 18 of them, rode out of the valley, crossed the river and moved up Greasy Grass Rise without making any effort to conceal their approach. The cavalrymen spotted them and took careful aim at the brazen group as they came across Low Ridge. Riding their ponies hard, the boys held a tight formation until they were less than 200 yards from the barricade. Then, in a sudden and beautifully synchronized action, they split into two groups of equal size. Half continued straight ahead while the others swung to their right. Their timing was perfect but costly, for an instant later cavalry carbines erupted and the first group of young braves was mowed down.

With the troopers focused on the first group, the second made it over the south end of the makeshift rampart. Unlike Crazy Horse's Oglala, the Suicide Boys did not ride through the position. Instead, once inside the perimeter they leapt from their steeds to stand

among the startled soldiers. *"The Suicide Boys,"* said Wolf Tooth, *"started the hand-to-hand fight, and all of them were killed then, or were wounded and died later."*

The heroic self-sacrifice gave the warriors still outside the chance they needed. With the bluecoats' attention necessarily fixed on eliminating the fanatic youths, Gall gave the signal for the all-out attack. The great Hunkpapa war chief himself led the way, as mounted combatants — concentrated to the east and west — thundered forward. Others on foot rose out of the ravines in a grand rush. *"All of the Indians…shouted and jumped up for hand-to-hand fighting,"* recalled Wolf Tooth. *"The Indians charged in from all sides."*

The mounted warriors streamed into the horseflesh bastion before the troopers realized what was happening. A few desperate shots were fired, but the converging riders simply ran over whoever was in their way. So much dirt was thrown up it became difficult to see. A veritable man-made dust storm enshrouded the hilltop. *"The dust was so thick during the [final part of] the battle that it nearly choked me,"* said Kate Bighead.

Like a needle through cloth, Gall and the others wove back and forth across the rise: *"On the hill there was a big dust [cloud], and our warriors were whirling in and out of it just like swallows."*

He recalled that the troopers no longer had much chance to take aim or reload: *"They shot away all they had…[then] the soldiers threw their rifles aside and fought with pistols."* Like many others, he closed in and showed no mercy: *"I killed a great many. I killed them with my hatchet; I did not use a gun."*

Indian casualties also were piling up. Among them was a Cheyenne named Bearded Man who was killed as he galloped through. An Oglala, Standing Bear, also fell amid the hurricane battle, but lived to tell his tale: *"I could see warriors flying around me like shadows. And the noise from the horses and guns, and the cries, were so loud it seemed quiet in there. And the voices seemed to be on top of the clouds. There were so many of us that I think we did not need guns; just the horses would have been enough."*

Having thrown the soldiers off balance, the mounted warriors withdrew as those on foot began to arrive. Storming in together, they hurled themselves into close-quarters combat. Said Wolf Tooth: *"The Indians were behind and among them. Some soldiers started to run…but they were killed before they got far."*

The dust and smoke became almost blinding. Within the deadly, nightmarish mayhem it was some-

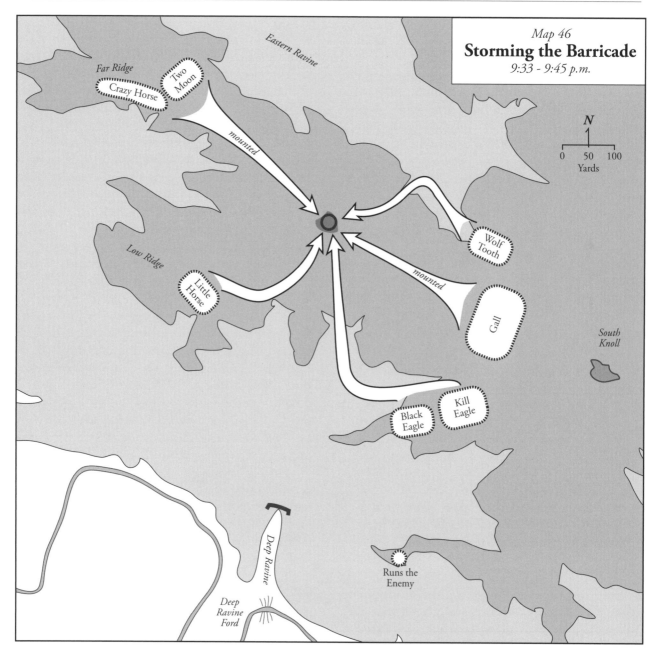

Map 46
Storming the Barricade
9:33 - 9:45 p.m.

times impossible to distinguish friend from foe. From a distance the last stand *"looked like a thousand dogs might look if they were all mixed together in a fight,"* recalled Standing Bear. *"The soldiers and Indians were all mixed up and a great many guns were going off."*

The fighting was desperate, bloody and brutal. Standing Bear continued: *"At the end it was quite a mess. The fighting was really close and they were shooting in every direction without taking aim…After they emptied their pistols…there was no time to reload. Neither side did. But most of the Indians had clubs or hatchets, while the soldiers just had guns. They would use those to hit and smash the enemy down."*

In that way the bluecoats fought and fell before the Indian avalanche. One warrior was seen charging a soldier who was holding his rifle by the barrel and swung it so hard he not only knocked down the brave but fell over as well. Joseph White Cow Bull, who had been in the battle from the very beginning, recalled seeing an officer, perhaps adjutant William Cooke:

One soldier still alive toward the last, wore a buckskin coat with fringes on it. I thought this man was the leader of the soldiers because he had ridden ahead of all the attackers as they came along the ridge. He saw me and shot at me twice with his re-

A more traditional rendering of the final moments.

volver, missing both times. I raised my rifle and fired at him. He went down. Then I saw another soldier crawl over to him. The leader was dead.

Among the last to perish was a trooper standing near the top of the hill within the inner defense ring, who was over-powered and pulled down by two Indians.

Quite suddenly, before anyone had time to see it coming, the fight seemed over. Looking around and seeing not a single white man left upright, the warriors vacated the barricade, then turned to wait for the air to clear. Even as they did so it became evident they had been mistaken; so the mounted hostiles went back in. Once again a churning cauldron of dust rose as they charged into the position, utterly crushing the last resistance on the blood-soaked summit. *"When the last soldier was killed,"* said Runs The Enemy, *"the smoke rolled up like a mountain over our heads."*

At 9:45 the fighting on North Hill ended. As the Indians waited for the dust to dissipate, they heard the sound of more shooting down toward the river. Soon they saw their compatriots on the lower slopes coming under fire from the bluecoats still within Deep Ravine. A moment later most of the warriors turned against that enemy, leaving behind a sizable contingent to move in and finish off any survivors on the hill, which they did by 9:50.

As far as is known, Sergeant John Ogden of *E Troop* was the ranking man among the remaining 30 members of the Custer battalion. The ravine he and his men defended was a funnel-like depression, several hundred feet across at its head, narrowing into a twisting corridor framed on either side by steep embankment. It was there the final drama of the Greasy Grass was played out. Said the Minniconju sub-chief, American Horse, when *"we discovered that there were some others who had gotten off [the hill] the warriors charged."*

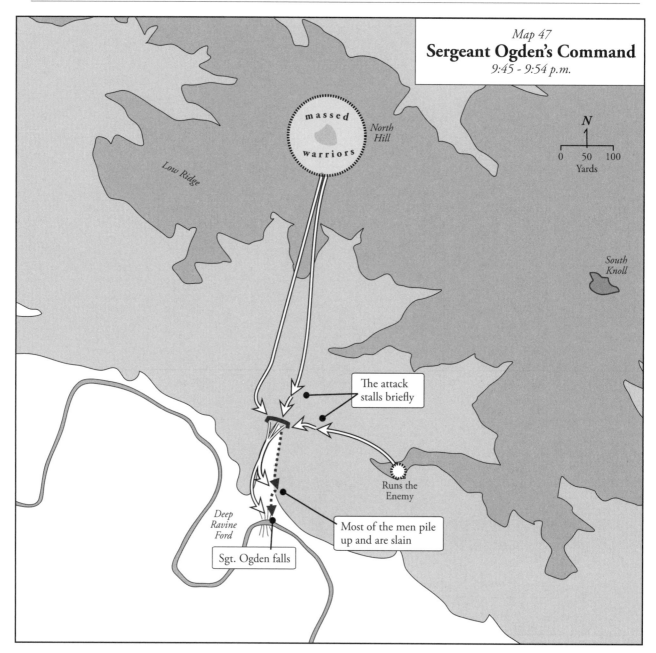

Map 47
Sergeant Ogden's Command
9:45 - 9:54 p.m.

massed warriors

North Hill

Low Ridge

N

0   50   100
Yards

South Knoll

The attack stalls briefly

Runs the Enemy

Most of the men pile up and are slain

Deep Ravine Ford

Sgt. Ogden falls

The defense line managed to hold for a brief period, but soon the left flank gave way under intense pressure. There was so much confusion the troopers on the right were not aware of that until it was too late; many of them ended up being shot in the back. *"We were right on top of the soldiers,"* said one participant, *"and there was no use in their hiding from us."*

Their ammunition nearly exhausted, the survivors made a rapid and orderly withdrawal toward the river. About 50 yards short of Deep Coulee Ford, their defense finally collapsed. According to a Cheyenne brave named Big Beaver: *"Fifteen or 20 troopers started to run*

down the ravine. They did not fire back, and the mounted Indians killed them. Those men were afraid."

All discipline disintegrated, and with it the will to resist. The few remaining soldiers ran for their lives along the lower end of the ravine, most of them unwittingly stumbling across and then dying amid the remains of the 11-man *F Troop* detachment massacred there more than three hours earlier.

Soon only Sgt. Ogden remained alive. Fleeing toward the river, he lost his life just a few yards from the bank of the Little Bighorn River. With his death, Custer's Last Stand was ended. It was 9:54 p.m.

Tatanka Yotanka
Sitting Bull
Head Chief of the Hunkpapa

Epilogue
From the Night of 25 June 1876

This chapter is an excerpt from
The Little Bighorn-Yellowstone Campaign of 1876
by Joseph Miranda
first published in Strategy & Tactics #236

Shortly after Sergeant Ogden fell, darkness put an end to the fighting around the High Hill, four miles to the south. The desultory siege of Reno's command continued for two more days, until the arrival of Terry's column. Rather than initiate another battle, the Indians broke contact. There is some debate about their motivation for doing so. Their position was not bad. After the destruction of Custer, and with Crook off to the south licking his wounds, Terry had barely more than 1,000 men under his immediate command. Estimates of Indian casualties at the Little Bighorn run from a low of around 100 to over 300. Though still serious by their standards, even the higher numbers represent only a fraction of the warriors in the area. Already well-armed, they were bolstered by weapons picked up on the battlefield: 200 or so breechloading carbines, with ammunition, plus many pistols.

Some of the more aggressive chiefs may have wanted to induce Terry to launch another attack and thereby surround and destroy another Army force, or even harass his command back to the Dakotas. Others figured that, with the destruction of Custer and his men, the campaign was effectively won – by white standards, the Indians had won all the battles, so the white should have acknowledged their defeat.

In the end, the argument was moot. Both Terry and Crook seemed content to laager their forces, and a frontal assault on a dug-in Army force was not in the cards. So the great Indian camp broke up, each individual nation going its own way (the Cheyenne even engaged in a tribal war against the Shoshone, who had provided scouts for the Army).

Terry, his campaign plan in ruins, let them go. A few days were spent collecting the dead, the course of the battle being inferred largely from their location. The final tally came to 268, including scouts and civilians, with another 55 wounded in Reno's command.

News of Custer's destruction traveled rapidly and caused a public uproar, though the actual casualties were light compared to the recent bloodletting of the Civil War. Congress demanded answers, and a scapegoat. Sheridan and Terry, seeing the way the political winds were blowing and facing the destruction of their own careers, provided one. Both Reno and Benteen came under scrutiny for their apparent abandonment of Custer, but more and more the disaster was put down to the impetuosity of their commander Custer's personality made the task of shifting the blame to him easier than it might have been, as he at-

tracted controversy even when alive. He had been (and remains today) one of the youngest generals ever in the U.S. Army, with a reputation for recklessness and daring. Then there were his politics. He led troops against the Ku Klux Klan in the Reconstruction South, and later exposed corruption in President Grant's administration. He was an active campaigner on the western frontier, where he established a reputation for ruthlessness against both the Indians and his own troopers (though the Washita was the only time Custer attacked anything that could be considered a civilian target).

He also became something of a celebrity with magazine articles and a book, *My Life on the Plains*. There was speculation he was planning to run for president in 1876, and that his daring actions prior to the Little Bighorn were, effectively, a publicity stunt (though subsequent investigation showed he was acting within Terry's broad mission guidelines). His persistence in taking the fight to Indians – foregoing several chances to break off the action – suggests something more than a purely military objective.

Outspoken, vainglorious, ambitious: Custer was a tailor-made scapegoat. In truth, he had made bad decisions during the day, mostly those that splintered his regiment into easily digestible portions. On the other hand, his conduct of the individual actions generally were excellent; even today, there is much to be learned about small unit tactics in difficult situations.

Custer could not have known – but might have been happy to learn – that his defeat would be immortalized as "Custer's Last Stand." Nor could he have known that, while the Little Bighorn would be the greatest battle ever won by the Plains Indians against the white man, it would become the turning point to their ultimate defeat.

For the Army, the Battle of Little Bighorn halted the campaign, but did not end it. It could not. Had the Indian victory gone unchallenged, it might have inspired other restive tribes to take the path to war.

Nevertheless, there were practicalities mitigating against an immediate resumption of operations. Terry and Crook spent July resting and resupplying. The War Department dutifully sent reinforcements, including replacements to rebuild the 7TH CAVALRY. The rejuvenated campaign resumed in August, with a much more powerful force.

In its early stages, the campaign took on a familiar pattern. Army columns moved into Indian country, but the tribes evaded contact. Most skirmishes, like that at

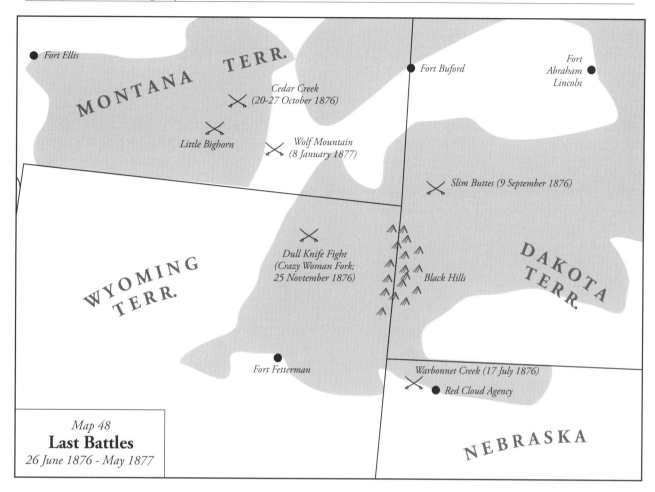

Map 48
Last Battles
26 June 1876 - May 1877

Warbonnet Creek in northwestern Nebraska (famous more for "Buffalo" Bill Cody's involvement than any effect on the war), resulted in few casualties.

A more significant success was scored in early September, when Crook attacked a Minniconju village at Slim Buttes in the Dakotas. Lodges were burnt, ponies captured, and Captain Keogh's bloodstained gloves recovered, but few casualties were inflicted. The return trek was a hungry one for the soldiers, as warriors under Crazy Horse harassed the column constantly, preventing the soldiers from hunting.

The Army would have to do more to win, and Terry had to win. He pushed his subordinates to fight through the winter, when the Indians were most vulnerable.

Battles remained elusive, but more encampments were destroyed. In October, Col. Nelson Miles chased Sitting Bull after a failed parley at Cedar Creek. Sitting Bull and a small band escaped to Canada, but most of his followers surrendered. The next month, Col. Ranald Mackenzie destroyed Dull Knife's Cheyenne village.

The last major Indian Band, under Crazy Horse (included remnants from both Sitting Bull and Dull Knife) was brought to bay by Miles at Wolf Mountain in January. The fight was a draw (Miles famously used wagon-borne cannon to stop Sioux attacks), but Crazy Horse recognized the inevitability of Indian defeat. In early May he surrendered at the Red Cloud Agency (where he soon would be murdered), bringing the war to an effective close.

Only Sitting Bull remained at large. He finally surrendered, peacefully, at Fort Buford in 1881, stating: *"I wish it to be remembered that I was the last man of my tribe to surrender my rifle, this day I have given it to you."*

Appendix I: Indian Witnesses' Names & Affiliations

Individual	Tribal Band	Status
American Horse	Minniconju	Sub-Chief
Big Beaver	Agency Cheyenne	Brave
Bobtail Horse	Non-Agency Cheyenne	Brave
Brave Calf	Non-Agency Cheyenne	Brave
Comes In Sight	Non-Agency Cheyenne	Sub-Chief
Crazy Horse	Non-Agency Cheyenne	War Chief
Crow King	Hunkpapa	Sub-Chief
Fast Bull	Minniconju	War Chief
Flying Hawk	Non-Agency Oglala	Brave
Foolish Elk	Non-Agency Oglala	Sub-Chief
Gall	Hunkpapa	War Chief
Good Voiced Elk	Hunkpapa	Brave
He Dog	Non-Agency Oglala	Sub-Chief
Horned Horse	Hunkpapa	Brave
Hump	Minniconju	Sub-Chief
Iron Hawk	Hunkpapa	Brave
Iron Star	Brule	Sub-Chief
Joseph White Cow Bull	Non-Agency Oglala	Brave
Kate Bighead	Non-Agency Cheyenne	Woman
Kill Eagle	Blackfoot	War Chief
Lame White Man	Agency Cheyenne	War Chief
Lights	Minniconju	War Chief
Little Hawk	Brule	War Chief
Little Horse	Agency Cheyenne	Sub-Chief
Low Dog	Agency Oglala	War Chief
Lying Down	Unknown	Brave
Mad Wolf	Non-Agency Cheyenne	Brave
Ohiyesa	Hunkpapa	Brave
Pretty White Buffalo	Hunkpapa	Woman
Red Bird	Agency Cheyenne	Child
Red Feather	Hunkpapa	Brave
Red Horse	Minniconju	Sub-Chief
Roan Bear	Non-Agency Cheyenne	Brave
Runs The Enemy	Two Kettle	War Chief
Sitting Bull	Hunkpapa	Tribal Chief
Standing Bear	Non-Agency Cheyenne	Brave
Two Eagles	Brule	Brave
Two Moon	Non-Agency Cheyenne	War Chief
Walks Lame Man	Cheyenne (Agency affiliation uncertain)	Brave
Waterman	Arapahoe	Brave
White Bull	Sans Arc	Sub-Chief
White Shield	Non-Agency Cheyenne	Brave
Wolftooth	Cheyenne (Agency affiliation uncertain)	Sub-Chief
Wooden Leg	Non-Agency Cheyenne	Sub-Chief
Yellow Nose	Non-Agency Cheyenne	Sub-Chief

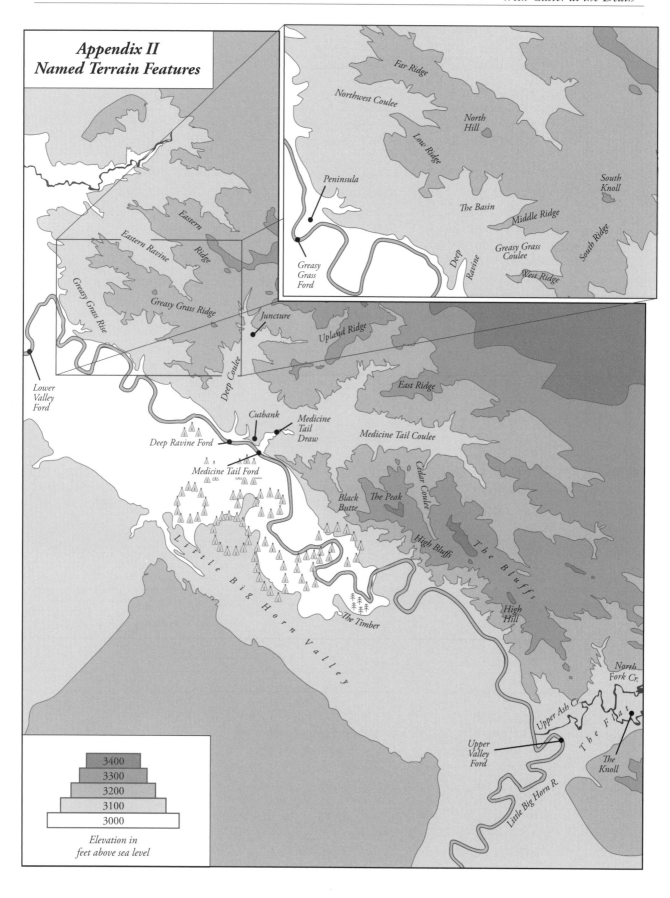

**Appendix II
Named Terrain Features**

Far Ridge

Northwest Coulee

North Hill

Low Ridge

Peninsula

The Basin

South Knoll

Middle Ridge

Greasy Grass Coulee

South Ridge

Greasy Grass Ford

Deep Ravine

West Ridge

Eastern Ridge

Eastern Ravine

Greasy Grass Ridge

Greasy Grass Rise

Juncture

Upland Ridge

Lower Valley Ford

Deep Coulee

East Ridge

Cutbank

Medicine Tail Draw

Medicine Tail Coulee

Deep Ravine Ford

Medicine Tail Ford

Cedar Coulee

Black Butte

The Peak

The Bluffs

High Bluffs

Little Big Horn Valley

High Hill

The Timber

North Fork Cr.

Upper Ash Cr.

The Float

Upper Valley Ford

The Knoll

Little Big Horn R.

| 3400 |
| 3300 |
| 3200 |
| 3100 |
| 3000 |

*Elevation in
feet above sea level*

The geographic place names in this book generally are those in use at the time of the battle. In other instances appellations made by Indian or cavalry participants are used, some for the first time. Where appropriate, post-battle christenings are substituted for earlier names.

Terrain Feature	Name's Origin	Present-Day Designation
The Basin	Indian	None
Black Butte	Indian	None
The Bluffs	Traditional	The Bluffs
Cedar Coulee	Post-Battle	Cedar Coulee
The Cutbank	Traditional	The Cutbank
Deep Coulee	Post-Battle	Deep Coulee
Deep Coulee Crossing	Author	None
Deep Ravine	Traditional	Deep Ravine
Deep Ravine Ford	Traditional	Deep Ravine Ford
East Ridge	Indian	Luce Ridge
Eastern Ravine	Indian	Crazy Horse Ravine
Eastern Ridge	Indian	None
Far Ridge	Author	None
The Flat	Post-Battle	The Flat
Greasy Grass Coulee	Author	Calhoun Coulee
Greasy Grass Ford	Author	Gibbon's Ford
Greasy Grass Ridge	Traditional	Battle Ridge
Greasy Grass Rise	Author	The Flats
The Heights	Cavalry	None
High Bluffs	Cavalry	None
High Hill	Cavalry	Reno-Benteen Hill
The Juncture	Indian	None
The Knoll	Post-Battle	The Knoll
Little Bighorn River	Traditional	Little Bighorn River
Little Bighorn Valley	Traditional	Little Bighorn Valley
Low Ridge	Author	Cemetery Ridge
Lower Valley Ford	Author	Sioux Ford
Medicine Tail Coulee	Traditional	Medicine Tail Coulee
Medicine Tail Draw	Author	None
Medicine Tail Ford	Traditional	Minniconju Ford
Middle Ridge	Author	None
North Fork Creek	Traditional	North Fork Creek
North Hill	Author	Custer Hill
Northwest Coulee	Author	Cemetery Ravine
The Peak	Cavalry	Weir Point
The Peninsula	Author	None
South Knoll	Author	Calhoun Hill
South Ridge	Author	Calhoun Ridge
The Timber	Cavalry	Reno's Timber
Upland Ridge	Indian	Nye-Cartwright Ridge
Upper Ash Creek	Traditional	Upper Ash Creek
Upper Valley Ford	Author	Ford A
West Ridge	Author	Greasy Grass Ridge

Index